I0152116

THE SERMON ON THE MOUNT

1900. Paris
Sédir

THE SERMON ON THE MOUNT

Paul Sédir

First published in French as
Le Sermon sur la Montagne
A.-L. Legrand, Éditeur
Sotteville-lez-Rouen, 1926

an imprint of Sophia Perennis

Series Editor: James R. Wetmore

For information, address:
Friends in Spirit
Box 931, Philmont, NY 12565

ISBN 978-1-59731-229-5 (pbk)
ISBN 978-1-59731-231-8 (cloth)

Cover Design: Michael Schrauzer

CONTENTS

Acknowledgments

The publisher is deeply indebted to the "friends" of *Les Amitiés Spirituelles*, who have kept Paul Sédir's books in print in French for over a century, and for the dedication of those who have nurtured the vision that one day these books might appear in worthy editions for Anglophone readers. We gratefully thank in this connection Piers Vaughn and Peter Urbanski for the exchange of textual materials many years ago that led to this presents series, Robert Ledwidge for his technical assistance, and especially Madame Zadah Guérin-McCaffery, who nurtured this same vision and worked towards its realization for decades. Her skilled devotion to Sédir's works helped ensure that Sédir's carefully crafted style has been preserved in these Friends in Spirit translations.

Biographical Sketch

Yvon le loup, son of Hippolyte Le Loup and Séraphine Foeller, was born on January 2, 1871 in Dinan, in the Côtes du Nord region of France. As a child, Yvon suffered the effects of tuberculosis, partial blindness, and a grave leg fracture that troubled him throughout his life. His mother, of Hessian origin, taught him German, which he later spoke fluently. At the age of nine, he made his First Communion at St Augustin's church, then entered the Jesuit school on rue des Francs Bourgeois, where he quickly distinguished himself by his great intelligence. Observant to a fault, he became a fine draughtsman and would have liked to paint. He was drawn to music, drawing, literature, and was extraordinarily dexterous with his hands. In due course, however, he was obliged to pursue a more practical academic course, owing to the influence of his father, an old soldier imbued with discipline who had little understanding for the refinement of this quiet child with lofty aspirations. And so, as soon a Yvon passed his academic exams (1892), he joined the Banque de France. He was twenty-one years old.

A few years earlier, in his late teens (around 1890), a profound shift in Yvon's orientation had taken shape. Not far from the Banque de France was an esoteric bookshop and publishing house (La Librairie du Merveilleux), where Yvon soon met the well-known writer on esoteric matters, Dr. Gerard Encausse (Papus). This led to a great friendship between the two quite different men. Papus set the young Yvon to work organizing his extensive esoteric library and introduced him to numerous personalities from the heady, even feverish, esoteric milieu of the time. One evening, he was taken to the home of Stanislas de Guaita, a nobleman of Italian descent who possessed the most complete esoteric library then in existence. Around this time, Yvon published an article ("An Experiment in Practical Occultism") and made his debut as a speaker on the theme: "Divinatory Sciences and Chiromancy."

In 1891, Papus had formed the Order of Martinists, based on the teachings of "The Unknown Philosopher," Louis Claude de Saint-Martin (1743–1803), and asked Yvon to collaborate. This fraternity took up the ideas of Martinez de Pasqually's Kabbalistic rite, and formed the first initiatory level of Guaita's Rosicrucian fraternity. In these circles, young authors frequently used pseudonyms. Yvon took the name Paul Sédir (anagram of désir), Gerard Encausse became Papus, Dr. Emmanuel Lalande used the name Marc Haven, etc. From the time of his association with the new Martinist Order, Yvon regularly published his work as Paul Sédir.

In 1895, Papus passed his doctorate in medicine and opened a home for the aged. This necessitated Sédir taking on the bulk of the esoteric-hermetic activities on which he and Papus had been collaborating. Every evening he gave classes in Hebrew and Sanskrit, the psychic training of Hindu fakirs, yoga, experimental alchemy, astrology, esoteric botany, etc. He also organized various research groups on related subjects.

Sédir was also much attracted to mysticism, and frequented literary circles such that of the poet Paul-Marie

Verlaine. Meanwhile, in the rue de l'Ancienne Comédie, meetings of the Martinist Order were taking place, where Sédir became acquainted with individuals engaged in experiments regarding which he would later say: "It is here-below that you pay the highest price." His alchemical research did, however, enable him to acquire an ever deeper understanding of the foundations of what is known as the Great Work.

All these early aspects of Sédir's esoteric life reveal an overarching quest for truth that always led him to first experience something before speaking about it. He had by now attained great heights of "secret" knowledge, and even power. But to his great good fortune he had the wisdom to detach himself from these as soon as he realized their worthlessness and danger.

⊕

In July 1897, Gerard Encausse arranged for Sédir (then 26 years old) to meet a most singular man, Master Philippe of Lyon (Nizier Anthelme Philippe), to whom he was introduced by Madame Encausse. Master Philippe was a remarkable healer whom Sédir and others in his circle considered a Christian Master of the highest degree. Shortly after this meeting, Sédir left for Lyon to spend his vacation there. Just what happened at that time remains a private matter, although Sédir gives some inkling of what transpired in his autobiographical book *Initiations*, and also in a remarkable letter of May 1910:

> Together with some companions, I have done the rounds of all esotericisms and explored all crypts with the most fervent sincerity and hope of success. But none of the certainties I eventually grasped appeared

> to be The Certainty. Rabbis communicated their secret manuscripts to me; alchemists admitted me to their laboratories; Sufis, Buddhists, and Taoists led me during long nights to the abodes of their gods; a Brahmin let me copy his tables of mantra; a yogi imparted to me the secrets of contemplation. But one evening, after a certain meeting, what these admirable men taught became for me like haze rising at dusk on a sultry day. We run after what we think is hidden, but know nothing of our own religion, though its dogma and liturgy are the most complete presentation of integral knowledge on earth. Everything is there in Christianity. The Hindu *trimurti* is neither the Christian trinity nor the Pythagorean ternary; gnosis and the gospels do not lead to the same goal. Read in the texts what is there, not what one would wish to find there. To see that we know nothing; to experience that we can do nothing; to verify that heaven is here within us, and that our Friend constantly enfolds us within his blessed arms—this is the lesson of Jesus. This I have attempted to say by publishing, among other works, five volumes of lectures on the gospels.

Master Philippe had changed Sédir's orientation. *His mission had been affirmed*. He gave up all the esoteric fraternities (and his various ranks and offices in them) in order to devote himself wholly to living and spreading the gospel. His commentaries on the life of Christ are especially notable in that he accepts the intuitive faculty as a means of approaching the Truth. Sédir's literary output was extensive. His best known works are from this period are: *Prayer, Initiations, Mystic Forces, Christian Mysticism, Seven Mystical Gardens, The Childhood of Jesus, The Sermon on the Mount,*

Some Friends of God, The Healings of Christ, The Kingdom of God, The Crowning of His Work, Weekly Meditations, and *The Incandescent Path*. His lectures and books drew many devoted students, and in due course a fellowship called Les Amitiés Spirituelles ("Friends in Spirit") was formed. This organization undertook to publish many of Sédir's books, and though it is much diminished, it remains active today.

Sédir died in Paris. Twenty years later, Breton poet and novelist Théophile Briant of Dinan wrote:

> On February 3, 1926, Paul Sédir died in Paris at the age of 55. The death of this admirable man, with his gospel-inspired heart, went almost unnoticed by the mainstream press, which was more preoccupied with crowning the charlatans and histrionics who were entertaining the public, even as international catastrophes were on the verge of breaking out. Apart from the chosen few whom this Apostle of the End Times had called to the Light, most post-war jabberers were unaware that one of the century's most eloquent voices was no longer to be heard. His was a forerunner's voice, the voice of a herald proclaiming in a wilderness of contentious crowds, a voice that had been devoted for years to spreading the gospel and, at the threshold of the abyss, was raised in dire warning against the multiplied prostitutions of the word.†

† This sketch is based on biographical materials provided by Émile Besson and Max Camis (close friends of Sédir), recently published in English in *Paul Sédir: His Life and Work* (Friends in Spirit, 2024).

Preface

THIS VOLUME is the second of five that develop the theme of my commentaries upon the public life of Our Lord Jesus Christ. Some readers, who prefer the refinements of intellectual disciplines, of clear and strong logic, and the order one admires in the productions of French inspiration, have often been surprised that I did not subject my commentaries on the gospel to its laws. I would gladly have done so, but I thought it best not to follow my inclinations.

I might add that it would have been easy for me to adopt this method, as wonderful and unforeseen circumstances had, during my youth, brought me in touch with a synthesis of knowledge next to which such great conclusions as those of Ampere, Wronski, Auguste Comte, and F. Ch. Barlet seem but fragmentary attempts. And anyone, having received these keys to prehistoric patriarchal knowledge could, I believe, extract from these anecdotes, sayings, and acts of Jesus all kinds of sciences, arts, and rules. But another fortuitous meeting, the happiest (since beyond price, and for which I feel ever unworthy) showed me that cognition is but an image, the mental world a mirror, and any system a limitation.

Thought is an edifice. It has its own blueprint, its foundations, symmetrical distributions, concordant oppositions, secret passages, reception halls, and ornamentations. Thought is solid, fixed, limited. Doubtless, it can sway people and be admired, but its very nature holds it in check, and even its supreme effort can never reach further than the virgin and frozen summit of intellectual knowledge.

Feeling goes beyond that summit, and from there springs to the heavens of eternal life. In that indescribable world, no law of reason has any effect. There a being receives the wings of the pure spirit and the gift of limitless liberty. There, the inconceivable and the impossible bloom forever. There everything enjoys an ever renewed youth. There love and absolute motion have dominion. There God is all: everything lives in God without intermediaries. This is the domain of Jesus. The gospel describes it to us: the entire framework of the intellect is shattered.

That is why I have not employed didactic methods in my commentaries. My aim has been to lead the humble and sincere reader toward the inexhaustible wealth of spiritual poverty. In the so-called lack of continuity of my descriptions, each soul will discover intuitively and directly the food it needs. The intellect, disentangled from acquired habits, will find revealing analogies among seemingly unrelated subjects. Then it is from within himself—through the ardor of his search, upon the rigor of his moral discipline—that the reader must expect to fathom, broaden, and extend his comprehension of the gospel. His master will be holy desire, because, while the world of thought is limited to the universe, Jesus Christ leads us far beyond. When engaged in pursuing him and following his footsteps, our only concern should be to employ all the penetration of our mind to know ourselves, and all the energy of our will to master our selfishness.

Precursor, Adversary, and Friends

MAN appeared, sent by God: his name was John. He came as a witness, to bear witness in favor of the light, so that through him all men might learn to believe. He, himself, was not the light, but his mission was to bear witness to the light. Yes, the Word was made flesh and came to dwell among us, filled with grace and truth. John bore witness concerning him when he explained: This is he of whom I said: He who is to come after me has been set above me because he existed before me, and from his plenitude, we have all received grace upon grace. For the law was given through Moses, but grace and truth came from Jesus Christ. No one has ever seen God. He, the only-begotten Son, who is in the bosom of the Father, has revealed him to us.

It was in the fifteenth year of the reign of Tiberius Caesar, when Pontius Pilate was governor of Judea and Herod was tetrarch of Galilee, when his brother Philip was tetrarch of Iturea and Trachonitis, Lysanias was tetrarch of Abilene, and Annas and Caiaphas were the high priests, that the word of God came to John the son of Zacharias, in the desert of Judea. So he went through the region about the Jordan preaching the gospel of repentance for the remission of sins, as it has been prophesied: Behold, I am sending my messenger to precede you, who shall prepare your way. It was of him that the prophet Isaiah spoke when he said: There is a voice of one crying in the wilderness:

Prepare the way of the Lord,
Make straight his paths.
Every valley is to be bridged,
Every mountain and hill shall be leveled;
The winding roads are to be cut straight
And the rough paths made into smooth roads.
And all mankind is to see the saving power of God.

John wore a garment of camel's hair and a leather girdle around his loins, and locusts and wild honey were his food. When he saw many Pharisees and Sadducees coming to his baptism, he said to them: Brood of vipers! Who taught you to flee from the wrath to come? Come then, yield the acceptable fruits of repentance, do not presume to say in your heart: We have Abraham for our father; for I tell you, God has power to raise up children to Abraham out of these very stones. Already the axe has been put to the root of the trees, so that every tree which does not bring forth good fruit will be hewn down and cast into the fire.

The crowd then asked him: What is it, then, we are to do? He answered: He that has two coats must share with the man who has none; and he who has food to eat must do likewise. The publicans, too, came to be baptized, and they said: Master, what should we do? He answered: Exact no more than what has been prescribed to you. The soldier on guard also questioned him: And we, what should we do? To them, he replied: Do not use men roughly; do not accuse anyone falsely, and be content with your wages.

The people were in expectation and all wondered in their hearts if John might not be the Christ. John answered: I indeed am not the Christ. Who are you, are you Elijah? they asked. I am not he, he said. Are you the prophet? and he answered: No. Then they again asked: Who then are you? What can you tell us about yourself?" He answered: I am a voice who cries in the desert.

They continued to interrogate him: Why do you baptize, if you are not the Christ, nor Elijah, nor the Prophet? John answered: I indeed baptize you with water, but in the midst of you is someone whom you do not know. It is he who is to come after me, the strap of whose sandals I am not worthy to untie; he will baptize you with the Holy Spirit and with fire. He holds his winnowing-fan in his hand, and he will thoroughly clean his threshing-floor. He will gather the wheat into his barn; but the chaff he will consume with fire that can never be quenched.

⊕

Then Jesus came from Nazareth in Galilee and stood before John, at the Jordan, to be baptized by him. John, seeing him come to him, said: Here is the Lamb of God who remits all sins of the world. It is he of whom I said: "One is coming after me, who takes rank before me; he was when I was not; I myself did not know who he was, although the very reason why I

> have come, with my baptism of water, is to make him known to Israel.
>
> John objected to baptizing Jesus, saying: It is I who ought to be baptized by you, yet it is you who comes to me! Jesus answered: Let it be so for the present, it is well that we should fulfill all due observance. Then John gave way to him. When Jesus had been baptized, he came out of the water; and as he was praying, suddenly heaven was opened and the Spirit of God came down upon him, in the shape of a dove. A voice came from heaven and said: "You are my beloved Son in whom I am well-pleased."[1]

John the Baptist was sent by God to fulfill the prophecy of the prophet Isaiah, by announcing a baptism whereby men might repent. We might truly state that any man, any being, is an envoy of God, since all beings, having been created by him since the beginning, are the forms of his designs and the signs of his perfection. But, caught in a moment of time, upon a dot in space, these creatures do not show their primal face anymore. Buried beneath a thousand veils, marked by a thousand scars, all dusty from the secular roads they are traveling upon, beneath their indistinct silhouettes, one can distinguish but two or three of the secondary hands that guide them. At long intervals only, when one of these tired hordes reaches a decisive crossroad, God delegates an extraordinary guide, who, descending in a straight line directly from the eternal summits, comes deservedly as his authentic envoy.

[1] Matthew 3:1–12; Mark 1:2–8; Luke 3:1–18; John 1:6–8, 15–18; John 1:19–27; Matthew 3:13–17; Mark 1:9–11; Luke 3:21–22; John 1:29–34.

St Luke says: "The Word came upon John." It is the Son whom the Father assigns to him. Every activity of the Father is the Son, and as the Father's activity is incessant, the Son makes contact with all the beings within the measure they are capable of understanding him; and they bear witness to him within this measure. The missionaries also are singularly the most authentic and faithful witnesses, just like the Precursor, straight to whom the Son came personally.

The prophet and the fourth evangelist clarify each other. It seems as though the prophet tells what he sees in the future, and that the event is in preparation and will be realized independently of the prediction. That may be true for all that relates to the ordinary run of things. But in the supernatural realm, in the realm of the immediate rapports between God and man, it is on the contrary the prophecy that triggers the event. God sees, when he introduces himself, through an indescribable operation into duration (time), that on such and such a day men will need to be either encouraged or warned. A prophet transmits this message to them—and this takes place later, automatically, because divine speech is creative. Had the word not been uttered, the vicissitude would not have taken place. Let us remember that where God acts, there is liberty: it is, might I say, the regime of his adorable will.

God creates the world freely. He could have not created it, but once the "word" that sows stars is uttered, these enter into the regime of destiny and are bound to their own vital law. Later, in the course of logical development of their existence, God, when his love judges it worthwhile, intervenes to send supplementary and gratuitous help. He projects small, adventitious creations. Seers foresee some hidden consequences to the normal effects of natural laws. Prophets announce supernatural interventions, which, just because they are supernatural, do not disturb the equilibrium of natural actions.

The Incarnation of the Word is the most important among these divine aims: it crowns and sums them all. And John the Baptist—whose spirit formerly inhabited this spiritual comet issued from the inconceivable space of the unrevealed—had to come on earth first in order to prepare men for the vertiginous approach of redeeming love. He had to do so because Jesus Christ, the most formidable of individualities, is also a universe: he is the kingdom of heaven with its worlds and its angelic multitudes; he is a new creation; he is the unbelievable, the inconceivable; he is different from what any man expects. That is why, in order not to be repelled totally, he sends an ambassador to men, one who will tell what he has seen, and who, because he is a man, will speak their language, and they will believe him.

This herald will represent repentance, without which conversion is impossible. In order to take the right road, do we not have to recognize that we have made a mistake? Announcing kindness, he will have to be harsh; preceding pardon, he will speak of wrath; preparing fraternal joys, he will preach bitter regrets and tears; sent for all men, he first must isolate himself in the desert: both an inner and a physical desert. Valleys, hills, and paths in man's spirit, and, subsequently, geological upheavals, are all parallel: they are one and the same thing, like water that shapes itself to the form of the vase.

⊕

Creation is constructed in such a way that man finds himself living in the central part of each of the worlds of which it is composed, and his work consists in elaborating only that section of the world in which he lives, and of which he is fully conscious. The absolute is reflected in the center of all beings: one sees the unifying liaison, the axis that sustains both the planet and man, and, if the latter wishes it, the reintegration of the whole universe to its primal innocence into the kingdom of nature by means of man. Seen from this spiritual axis, physical and divine facts coincide. That is why the gospel must be contemplated as an autonomous organism, or as a system of realities that permits its homogeneous structure to be seen by the reader in the measure wherein he himself has made himself real, which means *one*: centralized and entirely permeable to the Spirit.

Thus, the desert wherein the Precursor prophesies is terrestrial life—luxuriant, of course, with jungles and temporal forests—but from the standpoint of eternity, sterile and arid because it is not the celestial Father who has planted these illusory gardens. Everything that comes from selfishness is seen in the invisible central realm as brambles and poisonous herbs. Charity—love alone—sows flowers, fruit trees, and spiritual grains. Just as, economically speaking, agriculture remains as the basis of public wealth, mystically speaking, our works are an immaterial agriculture. That is why Christ speaks so freely of fields, trees, and mountains. In these examples we see fresh allegories; but he, he simply relates how things are, seen through his eyes.

It has been correctly stated that the universe resembles an immense man whose innumerable vital centers or foci are connected to one another, just as our viscera are held and joined by means of the bones, muscles, arteries, and the arborescence of the nervous system. That which the doctors call arteries, veins, and nerves in our body, in the Scriptures are referred to as paths in creation. All beings are traveling along these roads, from the infusoriae up to the sun, and their journeys are their own particular lives. When these existences conform to the law, the paths are direct and easy; but when they are subject to their own selfishness, the ways become tortuous, stony, and rugged. Man, king among creatures, exerts a preponderant influence over them; they watch him act just as a schoolboy espies his teacher; hence, man is rigorously obliged to give the example of obedience and love.

In the invisible heart of the world, we are grouped as spiritual families. The large families are the less advanced; hence, they travel on the easiest and longest roads. There are some highly noble families that have only two or three members. There are even some mysterious men, the unknown Friends of Christ, who ceased having parents. Their crushing labor is known only to the Master; they cut a new path that the multitudes will travel centuries later. The greatest among men are the least known. John the Baptist is one of them.

The task of each common mortal is to level his own path, to straighten it out, and to cleanse it, so that on the last day Our Lord may appear upon it. A few rare disciples, a few saints, know how to cultivate the spiritual fields that border these paths. It is the great taciturn travelers, the solitary pilgrims of eternity, who map out the enclosure walls and cause to be built these mystical cities with their edifices, arts, sciences, and all their enchantments—of which the New Jerusalem is the marvelous prototype.

Mountains, precipices, and ocean depths are the proof of the subterranean wrath that shakes our planet; they are the corruptions, vileness, selfishness, and pride of its geological regimen. Its spiritual regimen offers similar inequalities, and the harmonization of these excesses depends upon the general conduct of human beings. Just as our vices sculpt our faces, the physical shape of the earth tells the state of its spirituality: someday she will attain the equilibrium demonstrated by the sphere, the geometric figure of harmonious perfection.

⊕

St Matthew and St Mark particularly mention the garment of camel's hair and the leather belt worn by the Precursor, as it had been Elijah's costume also. Later, Christ will tell the relationship between these two great servants. Let us be content with seeing a living lesson of penance in the simplicity of their garb and in the frugality of their food.

If contemporary mentality were not so avid of the superstitious and the fantastic, the cosmic power to which the camel is a support would be revealed, as well as the hidden virtue found in grasshoppers and honey. One would then perceive, with fear mixed with admiration, the severity of the psychic regimen that the ambassadors of heaven impose upon themselves, and the implacable energy they deploy in their inner struggles. I know nothing about beings such as John the Baptist. But whatever infinitesimal knowledge I might have, strikes me with a stupor similar to that of the mountain climber when he surveys the vertical walls at the base of which he creeps like a woodlouse at the bottom of a well.

John exhorted his audience to confess their sins publicly. It is a fact that any sin, since it is an injury inflicted upon some being, demands first of all the pardon of the injured one, then making amends for the offense. Such is the law of this kinematic morality. In order to satisfy it, one would have to find the injured one, as well as the witnesses to the offense, so that they might hear both the confession and the pardon. This convocation is impossible as a fact, unless one wants to await that the play of the palingenesis bring these dispersed persons together again. But at the time when the Baptist preached, it was the end of an epoch and the dawn of a new era. There was a great gathering of souls capable of seeing the light. It was time for the accounts due. Many old enemies, whether living or dead, in body or spirit, met face to face again in order to liquidate their old debts. The Baptist knew all that. He could read on anyone's forehead their somber, buried histories, and he could speak with the dead. He was not the judge, but the bailiff of the tribunal, and his baptism merely registered the conversion of the sinner.

He had the right to abash with virulent apostrophes all who heard him, because all of them had adulterated the law of Moses: they had transformed its purifying spirit into venomous formalisms; they all lived upon the bad instincts of one another, just as the viper feeds upon poisons and transforms her prey into venom. All claimed to have come from Abraham, but now they were his children in the flesh only; they had lost all spiritual filiation. The rabbis of that epoch taught the revolution of souls, just as the followers of Allain Kardec and the disciples of the Orient teach reincarnation today.

But then, as now, laziness knew how to take advantage of this theory; people used to send God the same insolent summons that demand a sort of explanation for our destiny: already we persisted in knowing the whys and wherefores; already we had the idea that if God does not give us a clear explanation of his designs, he can be neither good nor just. In short, already we were haughty, indocile, and disrespectful children. Neither will we be saved from the stones on our path because we have recited formulae mechanically. God can also bring forth faithful disciples of his Christ: were not the first Christians the outcasts and dregs of the Roman world?

Hence, the crowd was rushing to hear the prophet because the people had the presentiment of divine justice, just as snakes are aware of an oncoming inundation. We will have to speak of judgments quite often, as they always come, under one form or another, after the last exhortation of mercy. Joseph Flavius tells us that forty years after John, Vespasian massacred 50,000 Jews by the walls of Jericho. And the "mystical history" of the nineteenth century gives further proof that God is always prodigal with such warnings. Had the people of France heeded them, neither the tragic events marking the end of the second Empire, nor the 1914 War, nor what followed, could have burst into furor. Yet mercy never leaves us; it merely hides itself behind justice, from which vantage-point it watches over us, always ready to rush to our rescue. John gives us the clue when he says: "The axe is laid at the root of the tree." Though the sterile trunk will be cut and burned, the root will remain in good patient earth. Then, after a period of rest, some more vigorous offshoots will grow from it. No being returns to the original void.

⊕

Through such implications, men's minds were prepared for the coming of the One who, mightier than the Precursor, was before him, and who was also his master and ideal. The vision of the second John—the evangelist—explains the same fact by the formula: "I am the Alpha and the Omega." In fact, the Son is coeternal with the Father, since he *is*, as soon as the Father wills. And since the Father wills from all eternity, the Son is the original being: the first. On the other hand, as he is all the wills of the Father, and since the Father, being Lord of the worlds, will draw them to himself only when the total of his wills (meaning his Son) will have been realized—the Son is, then, the final being: complete and perfect being.

Hence, between Jesus and John there is the qualitative distance that exists between the whole and a part, between the perpetual and the accidental. If to baptize means to name, John, who baptizes with water, purifies his neophytes according to the earth. He cleanses them. He makes them capable of receiving the inner purification that Jesus will administer to them; capable of receiving their new eternal name, and of the regeneration of their immortal spirit by the Spirit. The first cleanses from material impurities; the second changes the essence, recreating and transmuting the self.

From then on, one perceives the economy of divine therapeutics. First comes the baptism of repentance (administered by men who have received the power), which opens the earthly personality of the disciple to the rays of grace. Then comes a particular baptism of fire, which one receives individually right after death, when one appears before the judge. Then another baptism, collectively given at the judgment of the race. And finally comes the last baptism, conferred by the Holy Spirit, which makes the disciple a free man and a citizen of eternity. There are still other baptisms, but these suffice as reference points to use in our contemplations. For each of them, the divine harvester cleanses his threshing floor, stacks the wheat, and burns the straw—for the harvest of races as well as for the harvest of individuals. Please note that only the straw is thrown into the fire: the straw, the support, the envelope, in short, the terrestrial—thus, no being is entirely lost, no being in his entirety goes into the fire that never goes out. The grain is always stored in celestial barns. It is up to us to see that our spirit produces more and greater grain and less straw: we will suffer sufficiently when the thatch burns.

This is, strictly speaking, but the bare minimum of justice being chained by mercy. The evangelist John makes us aware of it when he affirms that all of us have received of the plenitude of the Word gratuitously, without merit—we who are "voids." Nothing, even that which the greatest among beings has accomplished, can force God to come down: and he never can repay even that which he receives from him. It is God's love that makes his power obey; it is our love that, when gratuitously extended to our brothers through an inconceivable, adorable, and frightful absurdity, in turn makes itself obeyed by divine love. Before Jesus, there was Moses and there was rigor; Moses was shown the directives of the universe and their systems of equilibrium down to their smallest ramifications, even to those of the human body, even to the fractions of the dust particles of solitudes. This was the law: one had to obey. This was life in the barracks.

Jesus opened the gates, and it became the era of great open spaces and of the spontaneous zeal of love. Moses and his cohorts imposed diverse rules regarding hygiene; Jesus invites us to love first, because then our life, being spent in sacrifices, will subsequently far surpass the exigencies of anterior law. That which he brings us is gratuitous. It is essentially a gift, because nothing that is human or terrestrial can ever pay, or ever begin to pay, that which is celestial or divine. The law, on the contrary, offered man recompenses of the same nature and equal to the efforts he had expended: lights and happiness commensurate with his merits. In the order of knowledge, Moses also could only teach that which he had learned; while Jesus, coming from the house of the Father, artisan of all his works, teaches us truth itself. Truth is not knowledge, no more than intelligence is memory; we will later elucidate these points regarding other revealing words.

⊕

John the Baptist is not satisfied with mere platonic repentance. He wants acts. He is not content with repentance having mere self-centered effects. He wants useful repentance: one must share with the poor, one must act honestly, and never cheat anyone. We begin to feel the kind, simple, practical, and yet so lofty precepts that Christ will give us abundantly. The ambassador does announce explicitly the coming of his sovereign; and had the Levites, who questioned him, had the slightest intuition of eternal glories, they would have understood from his humble responses that an envoy so modest could only be the herald of the supreme Lord.

This herald, who was later proclaimed by his Master as the greatest among the children of men, does not want to be taken for Elijah, nor even for a prophet. He wants to be nothing but a voice, merely an instrument. He knows from experience that we are nothing unless heaven permits us to be something. Thus, in the sense of individuality, every human soul can become the bride of God, and the child that "she" (the soul) begets for him will be "herself" in her defining aspect of regeneration and freedom. The whole of all those souls united with the Word, living only for him as faithful instruments of his will, devoting all their strength to building with earthly substance a harmonious body for providential purposes, is the holy phalanx of the Friends, the inner Church—they are the laborers of the Master of the harvest, the soldiers of the Lord of peace.

In order to speak worthily of them, one would have to know them. But they remain silent; it is their works that speak for them. Thus, many people who mistake their aspirations for actions, wrongly believe themselves as belonging to these fraternities of light. It is not sufficient to know that Jesus is the only Son of God. It is not sufficient to aspire toward beatitude, or even to refrain from evil. We must have a living faith, give part of our own happiness to others, and we must serve for the good of all.

A definite hierarchy also exists in this mystical assembly. While all members seem to work at the same tasks, yet their value differs on many levels. The leaders alone are impeccable free agents consciously united with the Lord. The title of laborers and soldiers apply to them alone because they are the only ones who clearly see the cause, the methods, and the results of their work—from the beginning to the end. They alone are capable of total sacrifice. As a soldier offers his life, they too give up theirs when occasion demands. Moreover, they ceaselessly give their sentimental, their intellectual, and their spiritual life. John the Baptist was one of them—one of the greatest. That is why he dares state that his joy is perfect. Who has ever met a happy man? And to make us believe what prompts his incomprehensible rejoicing, the friend of the Bridegroom immediately adds: "He must increase, but I must decrease."

In fact, our happiness is limited because we only seek it in, and think it hidden beneath, what comes to pass. The Friend finds his happiness in what does not happen, he attains it by sacrificing himself. We—we run after a wisp of smoke untiringly, grasping after it with our clumsy fingers, which even deceptions do not deter. He—he places himself within unique Reality, abandons, gives, and lays himself open to it. Thus, in an ultimate dual deed, does he reach the absolute, plenitude, and perfection. Happiness is there: no jewel is ever closer to us, since it dwells within us. Why do we not imitate the Precursor?

Because we are nothing but of earth: we think of it, we speak about nothing else. And we are numberless. On the other hand, from above there comes but one: Christ. He is the first, the prince, the chief; so no one listens to him save a few, here and there: some dreamer who remembers; some jaded person who has lost all interest in money, glory, science, or in any god; or some simple soul who does not see evil. They are right, because Jesus brings us everything. His Father has given him everything for us. The Father always gives what is superfluous, or rather he offers it; it is up to us to take it. And taking the gifts of heaven means to believe in heaven, not only with our heart, but through action; it means doing the will of heaven. That is what lifts the arms of the man-spirit toward God. That is what fills his hand with gems and pearls. That is what permits the transfiguring waters of eternal life to flow as of now into our veins as powerfully as our perishable person can withstand. Then we can lose everything: fortune, friends, health, and power, since everything is repaid us a hundredfold in advance.

⊕

The declarations of John the Baptist did not seem sufficient to win over the people. Jesus wanted the prophet's embassy to receive a startling confirmation from himself. He wanted to authenticate this baptism of penitence. From the first day he wanted to give to all future leaders, bishops, and princes the perfect example of all the responsibilities that the superior is held to account for by God toward his inferiors. Jesus went down to the Jordan to receive the exterior baptism: he, chief of all baptisms, denominator of all creatures, voluntary penitent of all the sins he never committed...

So, he rejoins John between Bethany, site of grace, and Bethabara, site of the boat, the place of the passage: thus, between justice, distributor of ancient law, and the gratuitous favor of the new law, John designates him as the Lamb of God who takes away the sins of the world, taking them upon himself. Through a mystery in fact, that only his most intimate Friends have any definite notions about, Jesus, purity personified, has permitted a horde of impurities to spread within him: so that from now on, beside each temptation, poor sinners will find the virtue to overcome it; so that each of these poor humans will be partially acquitted upon paying past debts; so that in all auspicious or inauspicious circumstances, their spirit, whether elated or fearful, may emulate the impassible model of ineffable serenity and divine calm.

From the time of the Lamb, there has not been, nor will there ever be, any kind of test for which we cannot find the supernatural example given by Jesus, if we seek it with the eyes of faith. And this is true on earth as well as upon all other planes until the consummation of time.

But it is faith alone that introduces us into this mystery.

Let us first believe, believe in spite of logic, believe in spite of probability. Let us force ourselves to believe, let us grasp doubt and crush it, giving no heed to its whispers. Remember: the Baptist declares that he did not know him whose coming he was to announce. What unbelievable ignorance, and what a powerful embrace of the impossible. What audacious initiative on the part of this missionary whom one might have believed to be merely an obedient servant: "I did not know him, but it was in order that he could manifest that I came to baptize with water." Here is still another mystery: the divine order brought face to face with human acceptance. God designates one of his servants, and he commands. One would think that the latter has no choice but to obey, but that is not so, because he remains free to examine, and sometimes he refuses—for man is only a man.

Moses was indocile; Elijah was afraid. Yet if the servant obeys, his obedience, being a gift from God, is taken into account by God as a freewill decision. The Father's tenderness wants it so, in order that we may have the merit of obeying as well as the merit of shouldering a responsibility. I may be telling too much, or too little: we are at the moment traveling through the foreign land of the beyond into the unknown itself, into this universe that pre-existed reason and that will subsist after reason, but where one lands only after having explored reason to the uttermost.

The initial act of the public life of the Son was magnified by the presence of the Father and of the Spirit. Jesus wants to annihilate himself, so John prostrates himself before an order for the execution of which even the sublimest of archangels would ever be totally unworthy. Yet this dual folly of humiliation, which Jesus expresses forcibly—the justice of God—is the All-Justice, incomprehensible to our logic because it realizes the ineffable accord between the infinite and the finite. So John is the only one who "saw" the Spirit, and "heard" the Father glorifying his Son.

From the immense simplicity of this text, one could start speculating on the definite interconnections of the ear, of understanding, of faith, of the formless, of number, of the essence of vibration, and finally upon that of time and duration, with the Father. Also upon the correspondences of light, of the eye, of the atmosphere, of birds, and of space, with the Spirit. Many a brain is captivated by metaphysics and absorbed in such subtle researches. Our own domain, however, is that of love and action. We are certain that when it should be necessary, the Spirit will teach us everything in the twinkle of an eye, and that if we live the truth of the heart and the truth of the hands, the truth of the intelligence will be given us gratuitously.

⊕

Permit me to add a stroke to this sketch by transcribing a legend that the Christians of Lebanon transmit to one another. It may be purely imaginary, but I found that it opened a vista, and perhaps it will open for you a perspective upon the spiritual organization of our earth.

About six thousand two hundred and fifty miles away from our country, farther than Palestine, Chiraz, and Mascate, beyond the Indus and the frightening Bikanir, leaving behind the marvels of Delhi, rosy-hued in her atmosphere of gold—the traveler, passing the sites where long ago unfolded the enchantments of the Garden of Eden on his left, goes north through Nepal and finally starts to ascend the endless road that goes from Benares to the Tibetan solitudes, and on up to the gorges of Pamir. If he continues climbing toward the eternal snows; if, attempting the impossible, he succeeds to affront the unknown glaciers, and if the angels cut him his path, he will find an immaterial mountain barring his horizon, a mountain that even the liberated ones have never seen.

Surmounted by dizzying precipices on all sides, invincibly defended by its vertical cliffs, the murderous air currents die at its feet. It is this mountain that in the hymns of the Vedic Rishis is heralded to the veneration of the people of Bharat under the sacred name of Meru. Its dome-shaped summit curves into a verdant circle. A sun, still invisible to the Western peoples, maintains a mild, spring-like temperature, accentuated by wafting zephyrs. The ground is hidden beneath soft turf strewn with innumerable flowers, whose brilliance reminds one of the celestial gardens where the blessed sing.[2]

In the center of this immense meadow is a lake, in the middle of which reposes an island. The miraculous transparency of the water delicately reflects the grasses of the banks and the elegant foliage of the trees by the water's edge. An imperceptible inner palpitation of this liquid mass communicates to the reflections the indefiniteness of enchanted landscapes. The multicolored rocks in its depths and the permanent blue of the sky above give this deep water the appearance of a mobile mass of emeralds, dark sapphires, and turquoises.

The island seems to float upon a circular mirror that reflects it. Its elegant contours, the harmonious disorder of

[2] The account Paul Sédir gives here bears a remarkable resemblance to what the Catholic visionary Anne Catherine Emmerich (1774–1824) describes as the "Mount of the Prophets."

the clusters of trees that adorn it, their graceful attitude, the brightness of the immense flowers interlacing through some of their limbs, the perfumed scent of the corollas, and the chirping of scintillating birds, all concurs in producing an ensemble of perfect beauty.

No insects are to be seen, but animals such as antelopes, stag, and sheep of elegant, incomparable forms stand with their fawn or silvery robes against the background of the dark green meadows.

Towers, almost covered by gigantic climbing vines are hidden behind tall trees; multitudinous setting suns have tinted them with their purples and golds throughout the centuries. Some of the towers are round, others polygonal. Their divinely-proportioned measurements would enrapture the builders of the Acropolis. The stones do not seem to be jointed, but are like columns of marble or porphyry rising directly from the rocky soil. These are tombs. Below their base are to be found the remains of the antediluvian patriarchs: their place, their form, and their color represent the very arcana of which these patriarchs were the incarnations.

Numbering twenty-four and arranged in a circle, they mount guard around a sort of long tent or dais in the center, made of sumptuous cloth, which certainly seems to be the work of patient elemental spirits who weave the robes of angels. The shifting lights of the Aurora Borealis have impregnated it with their magnificent tints. This material falls in noble and abundant pleats that seem not to be draped upon a framework, but suspended from several golden cords that the eye follows in the radiant air without ever perceiving the immaterial rosette where these cords are joined together.

Beneath this dais stands a long stone table covered with books and scrolls; and going back and forth around it is a personage whose bearing is startling. He is not a man like us, neither is he one of the phantoms that haunt funeral places. He is alive; his spiritualized flesh radiates with such intensity that, next to him, the most beautiful human beings would seem to be moribunds at the door of a sepulchre. From his broad shoulders a saffron yellow material falls in great pleats. He resembles those pastors, sons of kings, mentioned in Saracen legends. A melancholic kindness softens the glance from eyes that have seen all too much, but his forehead, as serene as an archangel's, is overshadowed by the bluish reflection cast by his heavy shock of hair.

Upon the table, coming from one knows not whence, papyri covered with writing are falling continuously, as if suddenly materializing. The man reads them over; then, after having copied out some passages in his large book, he burns them in a blazing brazier set level with the ground. At the other extremity of the tent one sees a sort of three-wheeled chariot made of hard, translucid substance decorated with hieroglyphic arabesques. Finally, under the table, one distinguishes a sarcophagus, where lies the body of a man resembling the mysterious scribe.

What is this lake, this garden? Who is that man whose sublime demeanor crowns the beautiful surroundings? What is this dais suspended from a star, this perpetual fire burning without fuel, this dream-chariot which seems to be awaiting its team of unicorns? Might it not be the invisible patron of the inaccessible Rose-Croix, the thaumaturgist of Mt Carmel, or Elijah having come back under the name of the Baptist, the greatest among the sons of men?

It is he, in fact. There he will remain until the end of

time. He collects everything that men elaborate as saintly in the fields of thought, science, and art. He throws into the fire that which is impure. Thus does he accumulate the treasures of the true and the beautiful that someday will feed the elect of the New Jerusalem.

At intervals there descends from the zenith another being in human form, who, like Elijah, is neither a body nor a phantom. His rosy complexion blooms with youth, but the long undulating locks over his shoulders are silvery. He does not have wings, yet hovers as if sustained by the thousand folds of a vaporous bluish garment. He is beardless. His features and his tender smile radiate peaceful joy. His divine hands hold his wrap, which floats during the rapid flights of his ethereal courses. And no mortal sinner could ever bear the unfathomable innocence of his limpid gaze.

It is he, the seer, John the virgin, the beloved, the adopted son of Mary. While awaiting the return of his Jesus, he traverses the universe, gathers the benedictions that the Savior is sowing so as to bring them to our arid earth. Then he takes from Elijah's book that which the other worlds can use.

A third visitor, Moses, appears also upon this particular mountain. The theocrat bears upon his face the imprint of the flames of Mt Horeb and the majesty of Mt Sinai. The horns of thaumaturgical power extend from his frowning brow. His athletic hand holds the pontiff's wand. Upon his chest shine the authentic Urim and Thummin, which he ravished from the Sun-of-Numbers once upon a time. With long strides, he walks in amidst the tinkling of sacerdotal bells, and the startled birds hush at his passage. He is of short stature, his titan-like shoulders fill his ample purple mantle. Upon his brow rests a halo of immutability. The energy that seeps throughout his gestures animates even the folds of his vestments. He is the living figure of action and will.

But the scribe, the seer, and the priest do not act alone. They are, so to speak, the circumference of spheres whose centers remain buried in the living glory of the Sun-of-Souls. They form three couples united in the most intimate collaboration. Just as the new covenant perfects the ancient one, just as within Christ the painful efforts of the just unfold according to the splendor of eternal joy, so behind Elijah stands Enoch, the seventh son of Adam, the inventor of science, who descended in a direct line from the Sun-of-Forms.

Behind Moses stands the priest without ancestors, king of justice, Melchizedek, son of the red sun. Behind John stands James, the other son of thunder, who contemplates and prays in the most hidden retreat. None of these six have ever been subjected to earthly death. Yet all together, these six are one being and one spirit. These three spheres are one sphere only. They are the form of the future kingdom of the Father, here below.

A seventh being contains them all, though he is quite distinguishable by the mode of his existence and the quality of his light, which he directs and employs as he thinks best. He goes everywhere. There is not a palace that does not open its doors to him; all peaks are accessible to him; he descends into all ocean abysses; he scrutinizes all beings down to their primitive roots. He takes care of all; he takes on all forms; he looks like anyone, yet he is alone on earth. Passersby may encounter him on the street; in their ecstasies, the saints see him as identical to eternal figures. His anonymous appearance constitutes his mystery, his defense, and his all-powerfulness. He is called Lord of the Earth.

The celestial waters that nourish all creatures come to them through Enoch and Elijah. The lights that illumine them come through John and James. The benedictions that heal them come through Melchizedek and Moses. And all the disciples of Jesus, whatever be their race, their rite, or their essential quality, belong to one of these three couples, thus forming in the invisible a complete world of lights, of living waters, and of scented breaths.

Finally, equally close to the site where, at the dawn of centuries, bloomed the delights of the Garden of Eden, but in a northern direction, rises another legendary mountain, where masters of perversity dwell.

The Temptation

HEN JESUS was led into the desert by the Spirit, to be tempted by the devil, and after fasting for forty days and forty nights, he was hungry. The tempter came and said: If you are the Son of God, command that these stones become loaves of bread. But Jesus answered: It is written, man does not live by bread alone, but by every word that comes forth from the mouth of God.

Then the devil took him into the holy city and set him down on the pinnacle of the Temple of Jerusalem and said: If you are the Son of God, throw yourself down, for it is written: He has given his angels charge concerning thee, and they will hold thee up with their hands, lest thou trip on a stone. Jesus said to him: It is written further, Thou shalt not tempt the Lord thy God.

Again the devil took him to a very high mountain, showed him all the kingdoms of the world and the glory of them. And he said to him: All these things I will give to thee, if thou wilt fall down and worship me. Then Jesus said: Begone Satan! for it is written: Thou shalt worship the Lord thy God and serve none but him.

Then, having tried all kinds of temptations, the devil left him until another time, and, behold, angels came and ministered to him.

Then Jesus began to preach and said: Repent, because the kingdom of God is at hand.

Passing along by the sea of Galilee, he saw Simon and his brother Andrew who were casting their nets in the sea. Jesus said to them: Come, follow me, and I shall make you fishers of men. Then looking at Simon, he said, You are Simon, son of Jonas, you shall be called Cephas (which means Peter, "the stone").

Going a little farther on, he saw two other brothers, James the son of Zebedee, and his brother John, in a boat with their father, Zebedee, mending their nets; he called to them. Immediately they left their nets and their father, and followed him.

The next day Jesus found Philip. Jesus said to him: Follow me. Philip was from Bethsaida, the city of Peter and Andrew.

Philip found Nathaniel and said to him: We have found him of whom Moses wrote in the law and the prophets too, it is Jesus of Nazareth, the son of Joseph. Then Nathanael asked him, Can anything good come out of Nazareth? Philip answered him, Come and see.

Jesus saw Nathanael coming toward him and said: Behold a true Israelite in whom there is no guile! Nathanael asked him: How dost thou know me? Jesus answered him: Before Phillip called thee when thou wast under the fig tree, I saw thee. Nathanael replied: Master, Thou art the Son of God, Thou art the King of Israel.

Jesus answered, Because I said I saw thee under the fig tree, thou dost believe! Greater things than these shalt thou see! Then he added: In truth I say to you, you shall see heaven opened, and the angels of God ascending and descending upon the Son of Man.

Three days later, a wedding feast took place at Cana in Galilee; the mother of Jesus was there. Jesus and his disciples had been invited to the marriage also. The wine having run short, the mother of Jesus said to him: They have no more wine. Jesus answered: Woman, what is there between you and me? My hour has not yet come. His mother told the servants, Do whatever he tells you.

Now there were six stone jars which were used for purification according to Jewish custom, each jar holding two or three measures.[1] Jesus told the servants, Fill the jars with water. They filled them up to the brim. Then he said to them, Now draw and give a draught to the chief steward. They took it to him.

When the chief steward had tasted the water after it became wine (not knowing whence it came, though the servants knew) he called the bridegroom and said to him: Every man at first sets forth the good wine and when they have drunk freely, he serves them that which is poorer; but you have kept the good wine till now.

[1] A measure being about 28 ½ quarts.

> This is how Jesus worked the first of his miracles at Cana in Galilee, and how he manifested his glory, and his disciples believed, in him![2]

In a previous book I have attempted to show the human and terrestrial side of the retreat of Jesus to the desert. One can also find therein (as in all the episodes of the gospel) a universal phenomenon, a spiritual drama, and a cosmic epic. In order to broaden and deepen our contemplation, it is necessary that our spirit be still more liberated from the confines of the personality, and for our imagination to loosen the reins of logic a bit more. Romanticism, which in fact takes root in the sphere of sentiment, only *appears* to be opposed to classicism. The latter, triumphing through order, measure, and reason only attains beauty when it reverts back to sentiment by the means of good taste. And inversely, through the same means of good taste, Romanticism digresses into detestable errors, if not tempered by reason. Thus does the human spirit oscillate between science and war, between theology and mysticism, between monarchies and demagogies—as, through vast alternate vibrations, it progresses toward the harmonious equilibrium expressed through the evangelical concept of the kingdom of heaven, where all of life's tendencies, and the desires of creatures, will mutually sacrifice each other so as to receive their definite, total, and perfect form.

Christ's fast is an example all should follow. It is the only one of the acts of the Master that the Church stresses and persistently commemorates. Why? Because it is the first vic-

[2] Matthew 4:1–11; Mark 1:12; Luke 4:1–13; Matthew 4:12–22; Mark 1:14–20; John 1:35–51, 2:1–11.

tory of the great war led by him against the enemy of humankind here below. Because it contains all the tactical and strategic lessons of our individual war against the minions of evil. And finally, because we too will have to duplicate it for our own account, after having received the baptism of the Spirit when on the verge of becoming free men.

⊕

The human personality of Christ is composed of all the pure sparks that reside within the center of all beings as permanent principles, as monitors or witnesses to all forms of existence. The spiritual task of Christ was to carry this immense flame of light and truth to the very limits of all spheres, so it would meet with the frozen fire of darkness and of error that permeates the person of the Adversary. In the human being, between the impeccable, impassible, and eternal soul, and the passive, inert body *per se*, lies the spirit, which is a complex and unseizable organism, a receptacle to all influences, ready for any possibility, and whose conscious personality actually forms but one tiny part thereof. It is this spirit (approximative image of the third divine Person) that struggles, suffers, merits, and demerits. It is this spirit that at decisive moments takes the self into the immaterial desert for purification and to meet temptation. It is this spirit that also gives witness of the light to the body and to the material world. It is this spirit that adapts the splendors of the soul to the earth and elevates up to heaven the obscure, unknown energies of the world and of physical beings, by transmuting them.

In order to triumph in this battle, it is essential for the self to abandon all creatures, and to keep away from all relations with the created: this is the solitude of the desert and the perfect "forty days' fast." If the first temptation sways our confidence in God, it means that our spirit derives its real strength from above only; it means that our spirit comes from above, and not from below: it is the halo of the soul that it must hold closely. By separating itself from God, the spirit committed the original sin: it will accomplish the terminal virtue by rebinding itself to God forever. Let us note here that the Devil attacks the very principle of spiritual life by holding out to us the grossest bait—that which belongs to material life. Let us note his tactics.

When this failed, he launches his efforts in the opposite direction: exaggerating this same confidence in God. Not having personally succeeded in making Jesus fall, he uses a ruse so that Jesus will fall of himself by inciting him to tempt God. To put God in the position of having to produce a miracle to get us out of peril is a sign of immeasurable pride. The only sinner whom heaven abandons to his own resources is the proud person.

Finally, in the third temptation are embodied all the cupidities. Wealth, power, and temporal glory are all subject to Satan, but they do not belong to him: they are his tools, his baits and bird-calls. When we get caught in those traps, the Insidious One immediately throws a large invisible net that he patiently tightens around us; and the more we fight, the more entangled we become. It is because the Jews could only conceive the Messiah as a powerful emperor that Jesus will call them later children of Satan.

Thus, having a desire for God, confidence in God, love of God; seeking God for our needs, seeking God in our sorrows, seeking God in our hopes and in our whole being—these are the elementary lessons given by Jesus. They are the practical and living lessons about things, the perpetual lessons that should be put into practice every day, as they would lead us to our goal much better than eloquence and scientific research would ever do.

⊕

St Luke ends his narrative by giving us two extremely useful ideas for inner development. The first is that the three temptations include and implicate all the others; and consequently, that the three powerful and victorious answers of Jesus can also be used for our little victories. They are definite and simple; and the Devil is very subtle and very cunning. The evangelist adds that Satan went away from Jesus "till another occasion." We see the Adversary beaten on all points, yet intending to return for another attack. Of course! Because the very basis of his character is obstinacy; it is obstinacy that blinds him, keeps him in darkness, and prevents him from changing. Because of obstinacy he remains the great negator and the great negative. Through obstinacy he pulls us backward, while Christ calls us forward through hope. Let us apply these remarks to ourselves and understand that our entire existence will be a perpetual battle. As long as we are too weak to work, then—except through the bait of possessions, of pleasures, and of temporal successes—we enjoy at intervals some quiet periods. And besides, we don't have dealings with the Devil: we belong to him, so he does not have to go out of his way for us. But when we have amassed enough strength to work for God, the more we understand the grandeur, the beauty, and the urgency of the task, the less we accept rest and the more we become for the Devil a coveted object, since we are escaping him.

Then, he *really* begins to bother about us. Ceaselessly lying in wait, ready to attack, he uses all means to catch us: seductions, fears, scruples, weariness, metaphysical subtleties, and gross materializations. And that goes on. It has to go on, and that is really the battle for which the soldier of God is ready. So, we little people who are still far from receiving this dignity, because the Devil does not pay us much mind, let us not become discouraged at our own evil. Let us realize that our first enemy is ourself; let us not get excited nor imagine ourselves to be saints: our task is evidently quite humble. All the more reason to do it gladly and perfectly, no matter how monotonous the returns may be.

I almost forgot the most pertinent fact, which is that Jesus and Satan speak to each other as two flesh and blood persons might. What does this mean? Is it a symbol, a rhetorical figure, dramatized fiction, popular superstition? No, it is plain reality. Jesus and Satan, the angels and demons, virtues and vices, powers and illusions, truths and errors, exist here and there as individuals, as wills, as bodies that are more or less perceptible to physical eyes as well as to the eyes of feeling and of intelligence. At this point we are referring to one of the problems of knowledge, of which the wrong solutions sow numerous disasters. These solutions abound, and are offered to us all dressed up, painted and perfumed, glittering or pathetically mysterious in turn.

These phantoms have been seen during other centuries, but in the nineteenth century they came to us from Germany: through Kant, Fichte, Beget, and Schelling, their poisons have spread abroad. The French philosophers have been infected: Bergson and Boutraux, to name but two famous contemporaries, always reckon with the *a priori* of subjectivism; genial artists such as Mallarmé, Rimbaud, and Villiers de l'Isle-Adam have enervated their vigor in these prestigious but unhealthy fogs. Baudelaire and Verlaine have understood the "real" better.

It is not true that thought is the only reality. One cannot stand simultaneously in the abstract and in the concrete. These acrobatics always terminate with a fall. For Villiers de l'Isle-Adam, the world of feeling as well as the affective or soul world are illusion; thought alone, being self-sufficing, is real; the perfect accomplishment of action is this "inner moment" with which the common man does not concern himself. No one can extricate himself from the illusion that is self-created about the universe, says Maitre Janus. He also said: "You are merely what you think." This point of view shows but one face of truth. Moreover, it is misinterpreting Ignatius of Loyola to accuse him of being a forerunner of Hegel, a Buddhist, or an autodidact Taoist when he recommends that to acquire faith one must outwardly make all the gestures of faith. The founder of the Jesuits only gave a process or a psychological angle.

Mallarmé agrees with Villiers de l'Isle-Adam when he says in his *Divagations*: "Why should words accomplish the marvel of explaining a fact of nature, if by that very vibration the fact vanishes away? It would be better were its emanation to express a pure notion, or rather arrive at making this pure notion felt." Mallarmé is aiming at the idea-flower, at the entity-bloom, when he describes a garden to us. Now, if that were the only reality, why would the Word have descended among us? Couldn't he have saved us just by "thinking" our salvation? Why would he have bothered to answer Satan, his disciples, and his enemies if all he had to do was form an intention? And why Creation? Was it not enough for absolute Thought to think the universe? No, these men of genius, these great artists, these profound thinkers, did not want to look at Jesus; they only looked at the most concrete form of his work—Catholicism—and even then they only saw in it a method, a process, a kind of admirable artifice, but not a living organism.

It is false to believe that all is illusion. On the contrary, everything is real—but only *there* where each form *exists.* When our consciousness perceives forests, mountains, and seas, it is not mistaken; it does not reflect phantoms. When it enters into the world of feelings, the world of forms erases itself gradually. When it enters into the world of ideas and the world of invisibles, these are all real while our consciousness travels through them. It is because our sages (probably due to their human pride) have not understood the unilateral weakness of their own consciousness that they have bitterly erected this inept theory of divine-like abstraction. No matter how piercing their probing, it did not penetrate to the center, because they stood before God as equal. The proof is that they lived in bitterness or melancholia. Hence, they did not understand God. Their effort to keep away from the ordinary man (who is probably odious) or to surpass him was based upon their self. Yet it is Jesus who is the base and the summit. To feel Jesus is to understand everything. To obey Jesus because we love him, this alone brings us the august joy of the delivered ones. That is the true path, since joy is the normal and total unfoldment of all our powers.

But better stop my promenades. Each must discover his own particular goal. Everything is an actual fact in the eyes of the disciples; hence supreme acts remain unexplainable.

While waiting beside Jesus for the complete massing of our forces before the battle, let us look at the multitude of beings grappling with adversaries who are equally as numerous. Nature is but a vast temptation, and it can only triumph (by that I mean it can only develop) through an equivalently broad victory by means of the weapons of the Spirit. The very rapports of the Creator with us, the secret design of providence for us, is that permanent temptation.

A father wanting his sons to have vigor and alertness, also incites them to perform gymnastics, and gives them adversaries of equal strength: a few scars, a few scratches, are inevitable; but the final benefits derived outweigh these minor mishaps.

With your permission we will keep to these simple analogies. Let us not get involved with mysteries. And since an idea can only live when it incarnates into an act, let us be content with the ideas we are able to put into practice. To sum it up, none of our teachers has ever done any more than to realize his ideal.

⊕

And now Jesus is coming to the men who were seated in the shadow of death. He will go to the very end of Palestine, as far as the Galilean hill, scorned by the other Jews, but where all his disciples, except Judas, were born.

The first four were fishermen: Simon ("he who listens") will become Cephas (or Peter, "the stone"); his brother Andrew ("the man"); then James and John, then the fifth, Philip, fellow-townsman of Peter and Andrew. The name of any creature in his native tongue contains his whole mystery. But it is a closed science; we are not wise enough to be given the key. And all the speculations of the kabbalists do not even reach its boundaries. It is forbidden for us to enter into many places, because of our insubordination or foolhardiness.

It is here that we find the episode of Nathanael, the true Israelite "in whom there is no guile." Integrity is in itself sufficient to make the descent of divine succor possible. The ways of heaven are absolutely straight, direct, simple, loyal, sincere; their very rectitude is what makes them seem impenetrable to us, because we live in the kingdom of lies. But to Nathanael, the great inner crisis of knowing God came in a direct line: Jesus "saw" him under the fig tree; in return he immediately recognized Jesus as the Son of God. This is an example of the admirable spontaneity and suddenness with which we should know Christ. Then comes the marvelous promise, or liberality of love, that gives twofold as soon as we recognize him. The first miracle comes as bait, then, as an overflowing recompense, comes the revelation of the Christic world, the vision of angels, of their operations, of all these mystical hordes coming and going through the known and hidden worlds. This is nothing but the mark of the true disciples, the soldiers of heaven, the Father's laborers.

Their perceptions are being exercised and their consciousness lives upon the invisible kingdom of Christ and on earth simultaneously. The seers, even the purest, lose contact with the visible world when one of the aspects of the invisible world strikes them. But the "soldier" is beyond these occlusions. In the same glance he encompasses the angel (form of the will of Christ) and the physical fact where that gesture ends. In life, he lives as one among us, and yet to him the bodies of beings are translucid: he sees them not as auras, elementary spirits, or other genii any more, but, I repeat, he sees in them the angels themselves, the pure spirits that link them to the Word: universal center and eternal heart of the cosmos.

This privilege awaits us too, if we imitate Nathanael. It implies all sciences—knowledge itself—since it shows us the rapport of all creatures and things with the Word. It implies having all powers—power itself—since it permits us to truly act upon the living center of these beings and of these things in the name of Christ. There, one finds the true perfection of man and his permanent equilibrium: anchored upon God on the one hand, adapted to all levels of the relative on the other, we find ourselves freed from all the tense efforts to which pantheism and occultism invite us. No more external training, no more restrictions to certain parts of our vital powers in view of obtaining illuminatory fever! Everything becomes calm, orderly, harmonious.

Let us not become unduly impatient. That which in the meeting between Nathanael and the Savior occurred in a matter of minutes, may in the spiritual meeting fill a whole lifetime or more, since purgatory is nothing but another mode of living beyond earth. Our comprehension can only see the culminating points. Recent experiments in physiology prove that nothing in our movements or perceptions is ever continuous; there is a continuity of shocks and jerks that are very small and very rapid. So it is with our intellectual life: thought is nothing but the mental thread that links two isolated concepts. It is just the same with our spiritual life: all happens by leaps. That is why patience is needed, and why our will must only intervene in its own field: mastery of self, overcoming of selfishness, and doing violence to our nature. The miracle of Cana takes place at the beginning of the public life of Our Lord, to teach us explicitly that our will must never intervene in the answering of our prayers.

Here is what I mean by that. The response of Jesus to his Mother, which scandalized a great many sentimental people, gives the key to this miracle. The famous "Woman, what is there in common between us?" is the impossible translation of a familiar phrase that means, approximately, "this is none of your business." Were this translation correct, these words would still explain but the simple reality.

There was nothing really in common between Christ and his Mother; not heredity, not psychological influence, not any mental form. The old contemplatives of the Middle Ages rightfully stated that the soul of Christ passed through the Virgin just like a ray of the sun passes through a pure crystal, without any alteration; that it was the crystal which received from the ray a new and subtle virtue. The Virgin had been chosen among all women only because she was the humblest of creatures, the most dedicated to God, the most totally receptive to the Spirit, the most translucid.

That which follows the answer of Jesus completes the idea: "My hour has not yet come." Hence, his will does not enter into this transmutation, though he knows it will take place. What a lesson for our blind, fearful, and perpetual worries! Yes, God is always concerned about us; yes, he knows our needs, even the artificial ones; and yes, of course he does not hesitate to perform miracles even for such an unimportant thing as quenching the thirst of guests who have already imbibed too freely.

Once I was traveling with a soldier of heaven and another man, a foreign official. The heat in the train was unbearable and the functionary complained of thirst, whereupon we heard crackling above our heads, and in the net we found a bottle we had already emptied, now filled anew with delicious fresh water, which we drank with delight. Yet later, this "soldier" affirmed that he had done nothing, nor asked for anything. This was a second miracle of Cana. How often have we been the beneficiaries of similar miracles? We think of heaven so seldom that we are hardly ever aware of its silent solicitude.

However, I ask the reader to see in this but my own opinion, which I will not defend. I simply propose it, though it is not accepted unanimously by commentators. For them, water signifies the natural man, and the wine or blood of Christ is that which recreates it and brings it out from passivity up to spiritual activity; for them, the six stone jars are the six ages of the world that the Word takes back once they are emptied in order to fill them with eternal life—wine representing the latter, since Christ later will refer to himself as being the vinestock. All of which is exact according to some particular angles in various symbologies. But what I am trying to elucidate is the central viewpoint, or Christ's own attitude.

When a great personage comes among people, each category of spectators interprets his actions or his speech according to their particular trend of mind; but the intention this personage has in mind is often quite different from what others adjudge him to have. I do not pretend to reveal divine intents; that would be imprudence, sheer conceit, and foolhardy. But I would like to see born into the mind of the seeker, sufficiently enthusiastic to reject any preconceived interpretations, the presentiment of what Christ perhaps wanted to accomplish when he spoke certain words, and what he meant to impart to us as he performed certain gestures. That is the reason why these pages do not offer any didactic continuity. They are merely notes. A system is always limited. The gospel, however, does not fence in; it is as vast as the universe and eternity. The only objective for which a system may prove useful is the battle against the self, because the Adversary is quite limited. Yet even so, we must modify our methods of asceticism from time to time.

The Beatitudes

ESUS, when he saw how great was their number, went up the mountainside; he sat down and his disciples came about. Then, lifting his eyes to them, he gave this teaching:

Blessed are the poor in spirit; the kingdom of heaven is theirs.
Blessed are those who mourn; they shall be comforted.
Blessed are the meek; they shall inherit the land.
Blessed are those who hunger and thirst for justice; they shall have their fill.
Blessed are the merciful; they shall obtain mercy.
Blessed are the clean of heart; they shall see God.
Blessed are the peacemakers; they shall be counted the children of God.
Blessed are those who suffer persecution in the cause of right; the kingdom of heaven is theirs.
Blessed are you, when men revile you and persecute you, and speak all manner of evil against you falsely, because of me. Be glad and light-hearted, for a rich reward awaits you in heaven; so it was they persecuted the prophets who went before you.

Woe upon you who are rich; you have your comfort already.
Woe upon you who are filled full; you shall be hungry.
Woe upon you who laugh now; you shall mourn and weep.

Woe upon you, when all men speak well of you; their fathers treated the false prophets no worse.

You are the salt of the earth; but if the salt becomes tasteless, what is there left to give taste to it?
There is no more to be done with it, but throw it out of doors for men to tread it under foot.

You are the light of the world; a city cannot be hidden if it is built on a mountain top. A lamp is not lighted to be put away under a bushel measure; it is put on the lampstand to give light to all the people of the house; and your light must shine so brightly before men that they can see your good works, and glorify your Father who is in heaven.[1]

All truth need not be told, no matter to what it pertains. In fact, what is truth, if not the most precise exactitude with which we perceive a fact? Let us understand that there are facts of all kinds, and perceptive faculties of all kinds also. To my way of thinking, a theorem, an equation, a concept, an emotion, whether passionate, esthetic, or religious, all that which touch our senses, all that which we can love or hate, all that which we can invent or think, add up to being facts. But the phenomena, aspects, or concepts from which we feel no vibration are as if they were non-existent to us.

In order for us to receive a truth, it is essential that this fact finds within us a receptive organ, a transmitting agent. For everything is substantial: the subtleness within a painting, the meditation of a philosopher, are living things of

[1] Matthew 5:1–16; Mark 9:49, 4:21; Luke 6:20–26, 14:34–35, 8:16.

themselves, living beings that the painter's eye or thinker's brain humanizes and brings down to our horizon.

We must not expect to receive truth, as long as we are not pure spirits. The truth of each one, the truth of each order, is the *x* of an equation that is situated between our capacity of receiving, the state of the milieu, and whatever particular truth presents itself. Only he who possesses truth can offer it to us, and he alone who possesses it is himself Truth. Hence we can only expect it from Christ.

⊕

Let us consider earthly life: the life of nature and that of man. Those who seek to appropriate it and utilize it are the doers or realizers; those whose concern is to feel it are the artists; those who are concerned with understanding and comprehending it are the scientists and philosophers. The ideal of the first should be goodness; the ideal of the second should be beauty; the ideal of the third should be truth. The only Master who offers these three ideals is he who is the way, the truth, and the life: Jesus Christ.

The truth enclosed within each creature has its seat in the center of that creature. Hence, only our spiritual center could perceive it; and it does perceive it. But, since through our fault the communications between our spirit and our consciousness are lacking, it follows that the truth is as if it were not. It is the extensions, refractions, and materializations of this truth that the extensions, refractions, and materializations of our central spiritual gateway is able to see.

I think it quite necessary that these views be understood thoroughly in order to understand what religious teaching should be, and to comprehend the mastery of Jesus in this function. To possess knowledge, to know the auditor, his mental and psychic life, his physiology, his atavisms; to know the subtle atmospheres through which speech must pass (the invisible ones, that is, which may feel its immaterial radiations); to weigh the attitude of all these beings; to know what they will do with the light they will have received, the probabilities concerning their future—such are the most comprehensible conditions Jesus satisfies when he speaks to men.

Why was the first public discourse of the Savior particularly the *beatitudes*? Why is heaven particularly mentioned first? Why is the first word one of hope, and why is the first promise one of happiness? Because God is good. You know it anyway: or at least you think you know; but you do not. No one knows, no one has plumbed the depth, the height, the width of the love he showers upon us; no one has yet penetrated the labyrinth of his adorable ruse; no one has yet discerned its real presence. The Father does not send us intermittent waves of love; it is we who love intermittently. In reality, we do not love; only the Father really loves. He bathes us in his love. He saturates us with it. And if we really want to understand something regarding the relationship he maintains with us, it is his inexhaustible love that we must first recall.

In the logical domains of knowledge, exploration is complicated. But in the mystical domain, everything becomes simple. Forget the great scholarly theories. Let your common sense convince you that God did not build the universe through necessity, that he could very well have dispensed with creating it, and that, finally, if he gave us life, it was not for his benefit but for ours. Behind all pantheisms, materialisms, agnosticisms there is this naive conviction that we, as well as the whole worldly apparatus, are indispensable. This is erroneous. God is free. He is not bound to creation. He has no need of us. But he loves us profoundly; and he has built the worlds so as to send us to school.

Doubtless, the treatment may be energetic. But as to the details, the tenderness of the Son and the pity of the Virgin soften the rules, which spares us from the many "detentions" we justly deserve. Also, our sorrows become exasperated that we do not accept them freely. The descent of the soul into matter is an inevitable law; no one may be dispensed from it. But see what prodigies of help the Master showers upon us! He accompanies us all along the descent, as well as all along the ascent. He posts guides at certain points. He appoints angels to our personal service. He gives us hope. He ceaselessly speaks to us of peace, of light, of happiness.

That is how his first words describe a radiant future. But why eight beatitudes? Why not seven or twelve? The question is negligible, because it is temporarily insoluble. I do not deny qualitative arithmetic. I insist, however, that it is an inaccessible science. Certainly, you will find abundant considerations upon the symbology of numbers in the fragments of Pythagoras, in Pierre Bungius, Saint-Martin, Eckartshausen, L' Abbe Lacuna, and in the nineteenth-century esotericists. But it is still symbolism, merely meanings attributed to numbers. It is not the life of numbers. Who will tell us how the zero passes on to become the unity (the one)? Yet this would denote the first theorem of living arithmology. Let us modestly admit that our intelligence is still too dense to penetrate the profound aspects of reality. After all, do many among our contemporaries thoroughly understand an avant-garde artist? Or again, have many people understood what the 1914 War really was?

Certain seekers, unable to see the particular originality of the gospel, collect the eternal points of similarity that it seems to have with other religious books. I think that I have already underlined sufficiently this ideological misinterpretation regarding the life of Christ and his moral maxims. Another misinterpretation still widespread among free spiritualists is that the eight beatitudes are identical to the eight paths of Buddhism. Such an exegesis is superficial. Gautama, in fact, teaches that man, in order to be saved, must rely upon himself alone. Christ teaches, to the contrary, that man must harness all his energies to make himself capable of receiving salvation—but that, in order for him to obtain it, the express aid of heaven is indispensable. Moreover, the Buddhistic salvation consists in evading the formidable wheel of rebirths. For the Bhikshu, compassion is nothing but the best means of guarding against that wheel. For the Christian, salvation means to break the chains of sin, not in order to rest in sempiternal quietude, but on the contrary to join this supreme activity of free collaboration toward establishing the kingdom of God. Two theories that start from such opposite viewpoints cannot have coincidental consequences. Nirvana is a place; the kingdom of heaven is another place, at the antipodes of the first. Their paths are not the same ones, but (given that it is possible to go from one point of the universe to another) there are crossroads. This is how exegetes locate identicalnesses, but in doing so they mistake the letter for the spirit, and the temporary event for the general law.

Instead of speculating upon spiritual facts, would it not be more reasonable to *experience* them—or at least to experience the part of them accessible to us? Were we to state that the eight beatifying perfections indicate, for example, eight forms of equilibrium in the social order, or eight methods that lead matter to immutability, or eight biological modes possible upon paradisiacal land, that would teach us nothing. And in any case, you are surely not obliged to believe what I may think on such a subject. So we will merely contemplate those beatitudes from the angle everyone has access to—i.e., what they are in themselves, in ourselves, and how to attain that state.

⊕

Blessed are the poor in spirit. Everyone knows what *poverty* is. But when it refers to the spirit, the concept is rather confusing. So let us try to clarify it.

In French versions of the New Testament, the word *psyche* is usually translated as "soul" and the word *pneuma* as "spirit." The first designates in most of the passages either the vital breath or etheric body, either the character, the emotive or active center, and sometimes the mentality, intelligence, or thought. On the other hand, pneuma seems rather to designate the personality, the conscience, but rarely the double.

In Greek literature the meaning of these two words varies according to the times, both in turn designating the breath of life, the double, and the center of passion. Psyche sometimes indicates the phantom. Pneuma is occasionally applied to enthusiasm, and to soul force. It is also the name of the Holy Spirit. The same indecisiveness exists upon the meaning of the Latin words *anima* and *spiritus.* Recently, many volumes have been written in an effort to fix these translations, but nothing conclusive has been established. I will therefore try as best I can to clarify this nebulous affair.

The human being, as resumé of the universe, must contain representations from all parts of the universe, and a delegation from divine powers—hence, an eternal as well as a temporal part. The first—being the divine spark, the germ of mystical regeneration, the point of tangence with the absolute—grows by means of the food brought to it by the works and sorrows of the temporal part, which also serve to slowly build for him a body of glory.

Temporal man is dual. He is both conscious and unconscious. In conscious man, whose center is the self (seat of the will, germ of free will, the responsible entity), are to be found the physical body, the affective center (seat of feelings or sentiments), and the intellectual center (where reason works and thought develops). Unconscious man is that immense organism which functions from vegetative life up to those marvelous unknown faculties by means of which are transmitted to us the news of far-off worlds, as well as intuitions and enthusiasms toward an ideal; through them also come discoveries to the inventor, findings to a genius, and inspiration in all kinds of desperate circumstances.

It is quite evident that Jesus directs his exhortations to our consciousness only. Yes, he acts upon the unconscious being, upon the divine spark itself, but he speaks only to the self. The majority of psychologists claim that the motor of the will is feeling, and that is exactly what Jesus tells us when he addresses himself to our heart. What he calls our soul or our spirit is everything that is neither the body, the will, nor the intellect. It is that part of us which is the secret man, man the unknown. More analytical precisions would be superfluous, because the gospel is a manual for practitioners and not a treatise for theorists.

Please let me add one more thought so as to bring this to a focus—to a wise judicious study. God is not a tyrant.

Though our actual lack of intelligence results from previous disobedience, his kindness accepts us just as we are each day. He only asks us to realize his law in the measure of our understanding. If perchance the word spirit represents the intellectual sphere to me, then by applying myself to break away from the results of my cerebral labor I fulfill the precept. If the word spirit represents to me some deeper faculty, then it is up to me to rid myself of the conviction that this faculty belongs to me. And so forth.

Of course, I respect and admire the austere efforts of the great philosophers. Their inquiry and meditations, though they might stray, do elevate us. I also admire the energy of the great doers, for even when they are mistaken they launch a movement, foment life, release reactions for progress. But all these things, all these modes of existence, come from the one common source. I mean the self, which is the pivot of our consciousness, the source of antipathies and sympathies, the secret operator of good and evil, the depository of merits and demerits, and the entry where the forces and splendors coming from our immortal and eternal being descend. The self, finally, is the athanor where all the meager efforts of our mortal being are being sublimated to glory. It is the self that becomes enlightened or remains in darkness, that diminishes or develops way beyond the temporal horizons where it forces its organs to work.

The poor in spirit, the so-called spiritual poor, can also be the rich to whom gold means nothing, inventors who give their patents away, those who triumph indifferent to glory, and scientists persuaded that they are essentially ignorant. Do not conclude from this that any of these men follow a wrong path; just like us, alas! They have chosen the way they thought best for them; they are right in attempting to focus all their energy on the conquest of illusions, since it is for them the best way of finding out that these are but illusions, since in due course it will be this very same ardent energy they find again at the threshold of eternity. And in the meanwhile the results of their effort will have been shed upon all creatures.

Experience is indispensable for judging things properly. That is why life is given us; that is why, at first, we render an idolatrous cult to life; then despise it, and finally begin to love life as the most precious divine gift when, with wisdom, we discover how it should be lived in order to go beyond it, to surpass it. It is then that we begin to move with it without being enslaved by it. That is a deeper poverty of spirit.

More so than wealth, renown, power, or knowledge, selfishness is our cherished, fictitious treasure. Christ does not address the elite so much as he does the masses, the immense mediocre crowd—we who have small jobs, little means, and limited understanding, but are yet overly gorged with self-esteem, self-importance, and overestimation of our worth. That is why we are embittered, unhappy, peevish; that is why we are in our own little hell—a prosaic little hell, yet a hell nevertheless. True spiritual poverty must be understood rather as a lessening of the self than as a detachment from the energies of the self.

Let us wage war against our tastes, against the tyranny of our character, against the bile and spleen of our temperament. Let us become flexible. Then, soon, we will reach the state where fortune and status are unimportant. Christ always gives us the quickest, most effective, most certain method. That which it has taken me a half hour to delineate for you, with circumlocutions and detours, he tells to you in six words: "Blessed are the poor in spirit." These six words contain everything.

There exist worlds where joy and suffering surpass our actual capacity to enjoy and to suffer, just as certain stars surpass our planet. We are proportionately perfectible. Before entering into eternal peace, we will go through purgatories and paradises where our power of suffering and our power of love will increase immensely—will reach profound depths and vertiginous exaltations. Love will conquer us little by little; little by little our sorrows, though greater, will lose their importance; and little by little we will be dominated by the sole concern of serving heaven.

Such is the true poverty of spirit, this inexplicable state wherein the disciple smiles while suffering, and where he bathes ceaselessly in joy, just as if he were a feelingless body, or insensible flesh, handed over to executioners.

Both time and space always reduce all created splendors to dust, no matter how sublime they are. The treasures of the absolute alone are impassible. Needless to try to attain them directly by means of our human powers alone: we would only capture a few vagabond images of supernatural truth, beauty, and goodness. But, while working at our temporal duties by means of our temporal faculties, let us work also upon our inner selves, toward our eternal duty, by means of the eternal force of our soul, by love.

Let us not hate our body, nor despise our intellect, nor scorn the little power that permits us to feel and to spread beauty. A lyricist has said, "The body—impure groom of the soul." Yes, the body needs the soul; but I am not sure that the soul does not need the body more!

And, when comparing the sighs of contemplatives thirsting for an all-immaterial life with the ardent plaints of souls in the beyond who are crushing toward the portals of the earth in order to receive a body (and with what joy!), one understands how this poor existence of ours today is precious, and of what resplendent futures it is the obscure seed and certain pledge.

⊕

Blessed are those who mourn. The second beatitude concerns the afflicted. I would like to be briefer this time, and yet I see so many things that seem important and encouraging! The most common attitude one has toward suffering is to find some means of evading it. Those who reject using those means by which others could in consequence suffer, constitute a minority. Those who never complain are rare. Rarer still are those who find happiness in tears. But how few ardent disciples do we meet who ask the Master to send them trials? These disciples show courage and intelligence. Courage, of course, because, though aware of the utility of tribulations, we reject them by cowardice, and mask our eyes in order not to see the magnificent fruits the sun of sorrow has ripened. Intelligence, too, because if we consented to understand that patience radiates, and if we really loved our fellow man, we would seek work instead of shirking it.

The law of work is unavoidable, yet we do not want to work, or else we work only to satisfy a selfish motive. As soon as that selfishness infringes upon the selfishness of our neighbor, he resists, he defends himself, and from this, mutual suffering ensues. There are a few exceptional people who work unselfishly either to permit an unknown quantity of truth and beauty to be revealed to others or to willingly shoulder the pain of others in order to lighten their load.

Those people suffer far more than the masses because they want matter to accept a little of the spirit. Matter resents receiving the spirit because it wants to shirk it, not obey it.

If suffering purifies, if it confers upon us an unassailable shield of protective nobility, well and good; however, we say: "Why has God, who is kindness personified, not invented an easier way to lead us to him?" Have we forgotten that he has provided all manner of means? First, he implants his law within our conscience, then he gives us intelligence so that we are able to see, everywhere, what infractions of the law beget. He guides us, he exhorts us. In short, he sets an example before us. What other means would you suggest? Is there any other way left than to leave us to grapple with the obvious, palpable, personal consequences of our disobedience? In reality, these reactions that we term evil are good in the end. No matter how bitter it tastes, medicine is a good thing to swallow. No, we must not refuse suffering. We must not become insensible: our fallow hearts need deeper furrows. An artifice may defer suffering for a while, yet when the terms are due, the spur merely penetrates deeper. On the contrary, the better we accept it, the less does suffering tear us apart. Let us remember that we are essentially spirits. The spirit grows, radiates, and sublimates itself only through sorrow. Suffering is also a defensive reaction against a moral, physiological, or spiritual invader. We are the crucibles; suffering is the fire, the redemption, the shield of good—it is Jesus.

Moreover, all created beings and the stupendous army of stars, the legions of light and shadow, all of them are in the hand of God, subject to his will. Whether one will or not, it is so. And if perchance we satisfy our whims occasionally, it is because God is willing. The disciples of Christ, the only ones for whom I write, will understand that I am not trying to decide in favor of God, because God needs no justification. I will not evoke the unknown existences that all of us are living before and after this one (even simultaneously with this one) upon one or another of the stars that fill the zodiac. These are all possibilities, doubtless, but they are also superfluous and cumbersome truths, untimely as well as oppressive. Addressing myself to disciples of Christ, I want to speak to them beyond reason, beyond opinions, even beyond imagination. I want to speak to them in the strict emptiness of faith, in the perfect night of faith; I want them to seek after God alone in creation. I want them to repeat perpetually: "All that comes to me is fine; all comes to me from God." This is the sole road to beatitude.

How many men are there, who, knowing that the man they are going to help will be their assassin, would still help that man? One could count them quickly. Also, how many men, who, knowing the cause of their suffering, hence, knowing the result of the faults they could commit, would practice virtue without calculation, forgetful of their fatal science? Any knowledge entails responsibility, and to shoulder that load one must first have been schooled through suffering.

From the standpoint of eternity, there is no injustice. Apparent wrongs are absolute justice. And if we accept the fact that only self-aggrandizement prevents us from entering heaven, we will welcome all self-abnegation with open arms. Suffering eats into the self little by little, reduces it to pulp. It elevates us through prayer. It evokes God forcibly through our persistent invocations. Let us welcome suffering gracefully. I do not say seek it, because that is the saints' domain; but let us accept it when it comes. Let us not run at its approach. Escape means impatience, bad temper; it is a form of complaint. Let us welcome it as I said, as a kindly visitor, as a courier of God.

Suffering brings us unique gifts. Never will any asceticism, contemplation, profound intellectuality, or gigantic will power ever give us such precious ones. These gifts are true knowledge, the understanding and mastery of ourselves; also force and peace. The one who has become totally patient obtains a certain beatitude and intimacy with Christ. Purgatories enable us to ascend as high as they have precipitated us downward. We cannot become lost; the faithful Shepherd permits us to go astray just far enough so that when he brings us back we may love him more!

We cannot extinguish the light within. We can veil it, adulterate it, shade it—but still it shines, because it feeds on suffering. The marvelous faculties of our spirit that we term virtues are being built by it, little by little; they are a thousand, yea thousands of times stronger and more beautiful than those of our body, or those of our mentality. These are really forces par excellence. These are the appendages, the limbs, the senses and organs of our moral being, of our affective spheres, and of our heart; and the heart is—the whole of Man.

Suffering works and operates way beyond the conscious moral states—way beyond patience, resignation, kindness, optimism, humility; even beyond prayer. The more we feel alone, the closer God approaches. The more we yearn for him, the more we draw suffering to ourselves. The deeper we sink into solitude, the more we hasten and climb up the steep and narrow path; the higher we climb toward light, the more darkness pulls us back. That is as it should be, since victory is within us—we are predestined to vanquish.

And since it propels us always further into the unexplored regions of the soul and into the unexplored regions of nature, suffering enriches us beyond all proportion to our efforts.

Suffering also makes us comprehend our brothers. It engenders pity. It broadens and deepens our heart. It demonstrates, or rather shows, us the solid cohesiveness between all human beings (the billions of ligatures and links that bind them together to make them brothers), the repercussion that each has on the mass, and the possible miracle of general enlightenment due to one single imperceptible spark. The spirit of the truly patient being operates invisibly upon all humanity and upon the whole of nature. Just as in the past (in ancient holocausts) the spirit of the sacrificed animal would open the road to the collective entity of his species and serve as the foundation to the prayers of the people, so in spiritual holocausts the patient man, the visible witnesses, the invisible assistants, and the milieu are all purified, spiritualized, and illumined.

We are dealing here with the great act of sacrifice, with mystical substitution, and reversibility. We will refer to it later regarding some discourses of Christ that bear more directly upon it. The beatitude of those who mourn does not designate the cause of their tears, but only that they are afflicted, hit by the whiplash of some anterior act, or else hurt by their very élan of compassion toward ingratitude, toward malice, or anything else. It suffices Christ to witness someone moaning to hasten to encourage him.

⊕

St Luke writes: "Blessed are you who weep now; you will laugh with joy." Now is the time when I would like to speak of the mystery of tears. Let us contemplate with clear vision the march of nature and the movements of our own existence: both are subject to the same vicissitudes and develop along parallel curves. We see the first leave the most subtle sphere that can fill space and reach the densest and most inert state where life can subsist. We see the second, primarily a brilliant light saturated with the spirit, becoming darker by degrees, becoming torpid, hard even, to the very petrifaction where the hearts of misers and murderers finally stop. Once the nadir has been reached, one must reascend to the zenith.

The march is arduous; where will creatures find strength? "Come to me, you who are overladen and I will give you solace," answers Jesus. This call is incessant; the voice of Jesus carries to the ends of the world and is heard by all: something within the center of all creatures hears the voice of love. Their effort to be awakened, the few awkward steps they take toward the path—because Jesus is never very far—is called suffering. This flame, spurting from their obstinate hope, which does not wish to die, is suffering. This fire of ever tardy repentance, is suffering. And the closer creatures approach their Savior, the more difficult are their steps, the more hope shines, and the deeper suffering digs into and furrows them.

Our engineers have found fires that liquefy the hardest stones. Suffering, however, is an infinitely stronger fire, for it reduces the hard diamond of self to tears. Truthfully, it is the only road that leads to God. And since it leads to God, it is noble: thus, since our tears make our heart sensitive to divine action, they are beautiful, precious, and pure.

There has never been, nor ever will be, but one single being in the world who has suffered, and still suffers, without having deserved it—this is Jesus. The torrent of martyrdoms that sprung at the foot of his cross was to dig the way throughout the worlds for the Consoler, from whose visit we are all called to benefit. Jesus at his very first public discourse announces it: "Blessed are those who weep, for they shall be comforted"; for we know that suffering is but the convulsion of selfishness and matter that do not want to be transformed, while consolation is the harmonious peace the spirit instills within us when we have made ourselves his temple.

Each time fire sets one of the envelopes of the self ablaze, tears flow. Pain in the body is a fire, sorrow is another, just as contrition and repentance are: those are bitter tears. But there are fires of light from which sweet tears flow: admiration, gratitude, love, pure joy, prayer, and ecstasy are numbered among these joyful fires.

Our weakness, through our tears, obliges the All-Mighty to descend. That is why tears are holy, why one must hide from men to shed them: they belong to God. God alone has the right to see them. God alone has the right to receive them. We should never shed them except before him and because of him. For a disciple to weep for a personal motive is a profanation; it is prostituting something sacred.

Whenever sorrow strikes at our heart, no matter from what cause, then—just as when Moses struck the rock—a spring of pure water gushes forth. Springs of kindness, strength, and patience—how beautiful are the eyes that thaw before the Lord! As vivifying and refreshing dew, tears are avidly awaited by all of our arid faculties that desire fecundation: they are the rain that the seeds of the divine ploughman needs in order to grow. They are the wine of our weakness, and in the *aqua fortis* that will corrode the stone of selfishness; they are the blood of all greatness and the true force of veritable desires.

⊕

Those who hunger and thirst for justice are just as much the celebrated heroes of civic and social liberties as are the noble hearts who bleed upon witnessing the oppression of the weak, who rush to help the victims of ruse or violence, who intervene in fratricidal fights, and who die in a just war, or for an ideal. They also are the angels of mercy who dress both physical and moral wounds, who preach humanity and kindness by example, and who, finally, acknowledging all legitimate rights to others, keep nothing but duties for themselves. Man's justice is crippled from birth; no legislator can foresee all cases; no judge, even the most impartial, can enter into the conscience of the accused to disentangle his exact share of responsibility, nor weigh the motivating power behind a felonious act. Alone, the justice of heaven probes hearts and loins, the proportions between atavism and free will, and the series of consequences of the act through all the worlds. The justice of man is merciless; the justice of heaven is forbearing because it is master of time and can push its boundaries. Moreover, God does not punish. He loves us. He never feels offended, because man's insignificance never touches his infinite greatness.

The thinker usually pauses in face of the antithesis of justice and mercy, which is a natural and supernatural antithesis in the kingdom of God, where is no justice, since there is no law that compels. The inhabitants of heaven obey freely. They are incapable of disobeying. Love fills all their being. There is no mercy there either, as there are no delinquents, nor penalties.

In creation, on the contrary, justice rules because a law was promulgated. It rules because any infraction to duty, any encroachment upon the rights of others, breaks the moral, social, economic, and even physical equilibrium, for the slightest local rupture invincibly propagates and gradually jeopardizes universal harmony.

But, as no one lets himself be cheated without defending himself or without bearing a grudge, and as divine law is universal life itself, any infraction is a morbid ferment that decomposes and poisons—an antidote becomes essential to cleanse, then to heal. The remedy we mean is mercy. And the doctor who administers it is Jesus, aided by those "who hunger and thirst for justice."

The ancient races among humankind, who, like old people, have a yen to philosophize, admitted the doctrine of successive lives in order to explain the apparent injustices of fate that are witnessed daily. Without attempting to examine this theory, whose objective proofs are quite difficult to bring to a focus, let us state that it often leads to unhappy errors of judgment—and that, in short, Christ was right in not promulgating it. In fact, we see very few reincarnationists accept with resignation the apparent injustices they have to undergo. Yes, in theory they agree that we are the only protagonists of our ordeals, but in practice they are refractory. On the other hand, we too often see these protagonists of multiple lives coldly state, before the suffering of another: "This is due to his sins in another life; he merited this; he must pay his karma." Here again, the East has transmitted to us a warped light.

Christ, on the other hand, exhorts us to accept the knocks of destiny with resignation: first, because they are just, next, because we should be avid for justice. In parallel, he asks us to ward off these very blows aimed at our brothers, to entreat for the incomprehensible justice called mercy to fall upon him, and if possible to pay the fine in his stead, and to do unto him what we would like God to do for us.

If injustices occur in the functioning of the world, or within the little governing body that directs the affairs of citizens, neither revolts nor riots will prevent them from recurring. History, being impartial, demonstrates that they would only bring more injustice from the opposite direction. Submission to tyrannical laws, alone, kills them and brings about the birth of wiser ones. Merciful hands alone can cure a desire for vengeance or grudges. Only an innocent man who offers to take the place of the guilty one can regenerate that corrupt heart. We all know well enough that instead of improving individuals, penal institutions and reform schools further their corruption.

Though this vast universe offers the friend of God but scenes of more or less brutal struggles, a time is coming and a place is being prepared where opposites will harmonize, where antinomies will be solved, where enemies will drink of the same cup and break the same bread, and where the oppressed will uplift their beseeching persecutors and thank them. At the banquet of the Bridegroom, the reconciled inimical sisters Justice and Mercy together will offer the living bread of love and the wine of eternal wisdom to the children of the Father.

But for this to occur, one must hunger and thirst for justice. One must want to eat and drink justice. Justice is in fact a substance. It is the very economy of the kingdom of God. It is the very fiber and sap of the great Tree of the Worlds of the Eternal Vine. And our own being of light desires it because it is its own offspring. It is also the Judge himself. It is the personage that the Son will assume on the last day. That is why the best among us can only hunger and thirst for justice. They cannot feed from it, so they wait. They are consumed in the desire for the immense banquet where the gods and worlds, pressed against the posts of the eternal portal, just like little dogs, are looking on and waiting for the repast of the elect, of the millenary hungry, and of the gaunt travelers to whom all the desert rocks have refused the spring water for which they were seeking.

Those who hunger and thirst—the poor, the ill, the erring ones and the pilgrims; and also the two crowds for whom the bread and the fish are multiplying—are they not the ones who want to gain heaven's riches to recover the vigor of innocence, to rediscover the road back to their natal home, and those who pray at the bottom steps of the supreme altar? They are legions, they are two crowds in fact, since the letter of the gospel is a complete reality. It is in the name of one and all of these that the Judge will say on the last day: "I was hungry, I thirsted...

Blessed are the meek. The meek are the ones whose every inclination is directed toward goodness. Essential goodness is the constant disposition of the Father hovering over the worlds and peoples, over each and all. Because goodness knows the causes, it is patient with the effects; because it comes from the permanent, it is indulgent with the upheavals of the transitory; because it flows from the summits, it bathes all the hollows with an equal amiability; because it is born from all-mightiness, it fears no revolt; because it is beautiful, it encompasses all ugliness; because it is true, it gives courage to all despondent wanderers.

The meek one goes to meet kindness. He lives still in error, but senses truth; ugliness shocks his instinct, which is nebulously aware of beauty; it is through voluntary weakness that he combats violence; and it is because he had a glimpse of glory that courage comes to help him labor in the mire; and because he knows how all roads lead to the eternal, no backsliding curbs his patient and powerful kindness.

And so, no matter how far the best among men may be from perfect goodness, this effort is still the least impossible for us. It is because of this relative ease that the meek receive only an earthly reward. How great the difficulties must be to become merciful, poor, or pure, since Jesus—when telling us that only the Father has the right to the title of good—shows us the immense value of goodness? Veritable goodness, active, creative, daring goodness, which in laic terminology is referred to as humanitarianism, philanthropy, altruism, devotion, and benevolence, is called in religious parlance charity. It then requires the most sublime gestures and the most exorbitant sacrifices. It is not man who practices charity, it is God who does so, by means of man. That is why it was said: the Father alone is good. That is also why Jesus speaks only of the benevolences of the meek.

The meek are the excellent hearts who know how to welcome life, beings, and things with affable and candid tenderness. They are kind and benevolent, they are willingly obliging, cordially attentive, and their services are good-naturedly rendered; they always find an excuse for the faults of others, tolerate their opinions, and always offer themselves as referees to conciliate quarrels. In short, the meek have been cleansed themselves of all fundamental forms of selfishness; they have made their heart an altar upon which they heap, daily, the acts of their perpetual benevolence, just as priests of old used to heap the precious sacrifices so that the fire from heaven, the fire of love, has only to descend to set them ablaze forever.

This preparatory work, this intaglio and the casting of this mold, demands efforts that only those who have made them can appreciate. In fact, it is the whole antique ethos of Socrates, Pythagoras, Epictetus, and Marcus Aurelius—used here for the simple underpinning of Christian morality. During their time, those men were the structure itself, whose altitude Jesus has inverted. In his hands they have become the trenches of his foundations. The new Temple will be erected upon them by invisible architects and by angelic companions: thus will creatures be able to compare their nothingness to divine totality.

Because they are those who *are* not, none of their vigor and cleverness, their energy and sensibilities, their instinct or intelligence, belongs to them. Those are but instruments for their work that nature loans them at birth, and that they must return at death—not only in good spiritual condition, but ameliorated, purified, rectified, beautified, and regenerated. I said "in good spiritual condition" because although, yes, the body is aged at death, passions seemingly weakened, and intelligence vacillating, beyond fibers and cells is the vital force, within the heart is desire, within the brain is thought. These energies, like all the others, which I do not touch upon just now, present themselves before the just Judge, luminous or bedimmed, according to what the self has used them for: the self is the responsible one, and quite often offers rusty or warped tools.

But the principal cause of these misdoings is that the self believes it possesses these working tools. It believes it so well that it identifies itself with them. Do we not say "I am ill," when we really mean that our body is feverish; or "I am happy," when it might only be a perfume wafting from the invisible that our sensibilities perceive? In short, the self is the spectator, the controller, the registrar, the actor. Just as the instinctive center has no need of the body in order to covet the fragrances of the material world; just as the affective center has no need of the nervous system in order to love or hate; just as the intellectual center has no need of the brain in order to choose the ideas with which it thinks, so the self has no need of these three spheres in order to be, to will, or to act. Separated from them, it might doubtless lose contact with the sensorial universe, with esthetics, or metaphysics—but it is pre-existent to them, survives them, and is not dependent upon them. Of course, they are useful to it: it is thanks to them that it can fulfill its destiny, just as it is thanks to the self that all the faculties serving it will reach the glorious state of pure spiritual substances. The ones and the others can live separately, but to attain perfection, all of them must live together.

The common error of conscience consists of identifying the motor with the wheels. Whenever a sensation, a feeling, or an idea comes to us, the means by which we recognize that perception is the conscience: the conscience knows itself, and it is that latter concept which is the true self. It is in this inappreciable point that the immense energies of liberty lie dormant. But alas! it is of this scant point that we are so proud. It endows everything we touch with believable fascinations. The man "who made a fortune" imagines he owes his success to his clever business acumen, to his persistent work and thriftiness; he believes himself a "self-made man," while, really, circumstances had been prepared for him and the necessary forces for utilizing them had been loaned to him: at his death, nothing from these labors will remain his, except the ideal—high or low—toward which he utilized them.

But all that destiny gives us, whether happiness or sorrow, is always a sort of test; and happiness is the most redoubtable of these severe tests. In reality, each temporal advantage makes us so much the more duty-bound toward our brothers who are devoid of it. Consider: what would happen to us, were nature to hoard?

One must not keep anything superfluous. Money, time, strength, intelligence, affection—all we cannot use must be offered to friends, to foes, to the indifferent, and to those we dislike. We must share. We must welcome the unspoken request of inferior creatures and things, without expecting gratitude, without being disheartened. Each time a friendly gesture is an effort for us, does it not show that we are unaccustomed to doing it? One only does easily that which one does often. Just as a pianist's fingers after thousands of exercisings need no eyes to guide them over the keyboard, so innumerable attempts, painful to the least virtue, are necessary before it becomes an integral part of our personality, and before its initiatives can spurt forth spontaneously at the first call of circumstances.

When nature and her ministers, the gods of the earth, will see how carefully we make their treasure fructify, with what generosity we distribute its dividends, they will entrust us with treasures more important still. We fertilize the little domain in which the Master has installed us by being affable, open-handed, and self-forgetful. And at the end of our long and loyal tenancy, he will deed to us this bit of ground we patiently improved for him. Such is the recompense of the meek.

⊕

Blessed are the merciful. Mercy finds fewer occasions of being exercised. It is a form of kindness that spares the guilty his punishment and forbids us to be vengeful. It is the virtue that belongs particularly to the governing classes. When we are above the bottom rung of the social ladder, we have a tendency to think that only the inferiors have duties, and the superiors alone have rights. On the contrary, the duties of the latter are far more imperious than the duties of the former.

The first step of mercy is not to have contempt for the lower classes, but to treat the humble and subordinate without harshness, without contempt or arrogance, impoliteness or indifference. It means offering them that welcome which understands their lack of education, their lack of culture, and takes into account the grim influence of poverty. It means viewing their faults without impatience, accepting their shortcomings, stubbornness, and small tyrannies. Finally, it means also that virtues as well as vice must pass through the heart in order to undergo redemptive transmutations. This mercy is as vast as the world. It encompasses the whole of humankind, all creatures, visible and invisible; indeed, even for abstract entities it exacts a universal and perpetual clemency.

The second step of mercy is the forgetting of deceptions, frauds, thwartings, and offenses. It means totally erasing them from our intellectual memory as well as from our physical memory.

The third step of mercy is the state wherein it is impossible to feel an offense, not because we are beyond such scorn, but because we have become small, so small that an arrow misses its mark in us. The humble disciple is invulnerable, far more than the superman; his calmness (antithesis of Olympian serenity) is born from total confidence in his Master's power, and from unshakable love.

Thus "the merciful will obtain mercy." What does this really mean? Is mercy so difficult for the Father, or else are we in such need of it? Yes, we need it. Our conscience may not be aware of our need for it, but our spiritual heart, knowing this, trembles and implores. But our heart has seen the light, it knows how beautiful and pure mercy is, as against the ugliness of self; with anguish it adds up the few odd merits it has perhaps acquired and weighs them against its mass of faults. The heart calculates how much immeasurable mercy it will need—because we are sinning every moment, either by forgetting God or by errors in our zeal. We must admit that we are well aware of what we have to do, since the simplest notion encompasses all others. But we erase from our mind all these religious ideas that bother us. We do not want to think of God. And so, slowly, this accidental blindness becomes chronic, and we end by forgetting God. This forgetting is willful. All the good it has prevented us from doing is placed to our debit. And if we do not consider ourselves great sinners, it is because we dare not examine ourselves: we lack courage and frankness. If we had to make amends according to strict justice for all the evils and their consequences that we sow (the consequences being a chain reaction), our penal servitude would be endless, especially as we continually commit new ones on the path of this forced labor. That is why we have such dire need for mercy!

That is why grace intervenes from time to time, either through the ministry of our guardian angel, through the prayer of a free soul, or through the command of Jesus. This spiritual benefactor pays our debts, either through letting us share the benefits of his own merits, or through drawing from the inexhaustible source of the Father's treasures. Let us remember that such favors are always *gratis*. A grace is never an exchange. One has no rights to it. One does not merit it. Neither can we ever merit it. All we can do is prevent the door from closing against it. Keeping open the door facing heaven is such a difficult task that we must employ all our strength to manage it. Let us then exert ourselves with inflexible energy to being merciful, as we will then obtain, on the last day, according to Christ's promise—his Mercy.

St James tells us that whoever has not been merciful will be condemned without mercy. Do not conclude from this that being merciful to our brothers constrains the mercy of the Judge to descend upon us. No. For no matter how far we may show clemency, we are still short of doing our duty. Do not conclude either that we will be punished for not having shown meekness. The Judge of justice does not punish, he permits the natural reactions of events to take place. But if we show ourselves intractable toward our debtors, the Judge, in order to teach us how difficult it is to deal with a pitiless creditor, will simply hold back the effusion of his mercy, no matter how difficult it is for his tenderness to do so. But if we have learned how to forgive, if we have been able to smile at our offenders, then our own faults will be paid for by the treasury of light in our stead.

⊕

Blessed are the pure in heart. Purity is what is incorruptible, what has been through the fire long enough and profoundly enough to have extracted from it clarity, beauty, and simplicity. Purity is quintessence from the bloom, the shine, and the sublime. It is that which is unalloyed, homogeneous, direct, integral, intact. It is, in short, the spirit, the only fire that feeds upon its own self, inexhaustibly.

Continence is but hygiene; chastity is but habitual purity; virginity is but a purity of the body. All three are precious, worthy of praise, and of incomparable help to the will. Only those who are capable of turning their eyes or desires away from a voluptuous form, who can refuse or consent to the tempting inebriation of their imagination, who command their hot-blooded youth to quiet down, know what inflexible energy had to be deployed for such victories. Yet, the sixth beatitude demands much more than this. It demands an infinitely more profound effort, a constant resistance to its paroxysm, and a fixity of the inner eye upon God, a fixity one reaches only after diverse preparations.

To quote St Thomas Aquinas, our soul saturates our physical body so minutely that all the instinctive propensities of the latter become perverse as soon as the "I" complacently stops listening. Physical pleasures soil, not because matter is unclean, but because, being close to demons and darkness, its vapors trouble the conscience, poison the will, and cast a shadow upon the light within us.

Thus, a pure heart is the one that desires nothing from sensuality, or from feeling; that seeks no more joys for itself, or for joy's sake, either from esthetic forms or from contact with people or in abstractions of the intelligence. This is the first degree of this purity.

The second degree means to perceive God in his works. Beautiful landscapes, the innocence of dawns, the splendor of sunsets, the majesty of mountains, the infinitude of the seas, the charm of gardens—all are signs of God. The strength of a tree, the elegance of an animal, the conformation of a human body, the expression of a face, are all signs of God. The splendor of a poem, the greatness of a symphony, the eloquence of a painting are signs of God. Everything is a sign of God. And each man who begins to purify his heart see signs of the divine image everywhere.

The third degree of purity is to recognize within all forms the form of Jesus, to find in all phenomena a gesture of Jesus, to grasp at the apex of all laws a thought of Jesus. Jesus fills the universe. One meets him at every instant, in all places. He travels the worlds, among which are those to which our body and our spirit have access. And as he himself says: "Who sees him, sees the Father." This vision, in all preceding degrees, was vague and indistinct rather than general; it was abstract and speculative; it was the divine vision as seen by the pantheists and ancient human wisdoms; it was the vision of the Hindu ascetic, knight of the Vedic Swan; of the Liberated One of the Veda followers; of the Buddhist Arhat; of the Taoist Phap; of the Sufi Union; of Medjnour, Zanoni, and Master Janus. The vision of the sixth beatitude, on the contrary, is precise, distinct in each of its phases, concrete and practical.

Through it, when the disciple looks at a stone, he is able to see its rapports with the eternal Rock; when he admires a flower, he is able to see the great Solomonic lily, the vine, the fig tree and the wheat, the palm and olive trees, the reeds and the thorny acacia; when he encounters animals, diseases, devils or angels, catastrophes and the sacrificial cups, he is able to discern through their earthly form their correspondences with the great Healer, the great Exorcist, the great Martyr, the Master of one and all.

Such a heart, after yearning so anxiously for Christ,

becomes receptive to his radiance alone, and discovers its innumerable marks in a single glance. We—even the most fervent among us—we see God in a mirror, in the mirror of nature, where eternal realities are but reflections, where the eternal Face is inverted. That which is the most beautiful here below, dare I say the most admirable—even were it the most grandiose and the most admired thing on earth—is the least and the most common in heaven, and certainly the least precious to the Father. That seems impossible; and yet it is true. If the kingdom of God were but the utmost pinnacle of perfection of created power, beauty, and truth to its trillionth potency, would it not be but an enlarged part of the relative? If the kingdom is the infinite, the ineffable, the impossible, the inconceivable—in short, the absolute—does it not necessarily have to develop its incommensurable powers inversely to those of this universe, since the universe is finite, possible, comprehensible, and relative?

It is through striving for purity that one finally sees Jesus in the center of all things. And in return, Jesus gives to his contemplator the "high honor" of ignorance. Nay, he does even better. Since any gift of Jesus is a perfect gift, by giving to his follower a little of the limpidity and penetration of his gaze, he gives himself. And when the recipient begins, finally, to withstand this formidable commerce; though his eyes are still used, yet it is not he who sees anymore: it is the Christ-God within him who sees.

Thus, to see God is to see by and through God. The pure man has given proof and token of his innocence, of his innocuousness, and of his good will. No creature fears him anymore. They all know or feel that from him nothing but help or joy will come, that he is the friend of all beings and things. For such a one, all barriers of castes, races, and religions have fallen away. I do not mean that they seem identical to him, but that all seem equally worthy of his prayers and sacrifice. He is not bound by his activity anymore: he is free. In order to know, he need not any longer elaborate his thoughts. He simply addresses himself to beings, to the stone as well as to the star, to the demon as well as to the angel; and because there is no shadow left in him, his interlocutors must answer him truthfully and reveal their essential nudity to him.

⊕

Blessed are the peacemakers. There is a tranquility that comes from apathy or indifference. There is another that comes from stoicism and impassibility. The first is inert. The second is based on pride. Neither comes from heaven. What comes from heaven is always alive and fruitful.

Whether the troubles at issue be inner conflicts or outer misunderstandings, concerns to do with desires, anguish regarding ambitions, envious grudges, vengeance, or rivalries, one cause only engenders them all: lack of confidence in God. We are not convinced of his solicitude. We cannot conceive that his permission is indispensable to the smallest result. We imagine that we are on our own alone, whether we harass our neighbor or have to bear with him. We are stumped by the apparent injustice of our problems. We give undue importance to temporal things, which nevertheless pass away; and yet we hurriedly try to reach an end as if our eternal fate depended upon our small successes or our illusory setbacks.

One can give only that which one possesses. For peace to be reestablished around us, we must first establish it within us. Both of these great works are equally difficult. Long is the road from here to the kingdom of peace, and our self does not walk very fast.

War is all about us: in our heart, our family, in the factory, the city, the nation, within ideas, among people, between religions, even within each religion. How bitter and alive it is even in the little circle we live in!

How can we establish inner peace, and how can we settle ourselves into it? All we can do is prepare ourselves to receive it, to make ourselves, not worthy, but only capable of receiving it; to cleanse, put in order, and ventilate the chambers of our spirit so that it may remain there for longer and longer visits.

First, let us acquire *sang froid*, self-control, and calm. We are an intimate mixture of matter and spirit. First, let us master matter (by which I mean our instincts), then let us discipline our emotions, and finally, let us straighten out our thinking. Possession of self, serenity, peaceful contemplation, and impartiality are the columns of the temple of peace.

These four columns are set upon four solid pedestals. The first pedestal is called patience, which endures everything without a murmur. The second pedestal is the humility that always takes a backseat, only accepts the bare necessities, and tries to grant the wishes of others. The third pedestal is the constant prayer that we may do God's will. The fourth pedestal is the smiling, supple mood that does not become involved with what is not one's burden, is not affected by what happens, and becomes impassioned only for eternal things.

The peaceful man has no suspicions toward others. He is only worried about his own faults. He welcomes beings and things benevolently, and receives the bores, the sympathetic people, joys and sorrows, with equal calm. His concern is with what lies above. He permits nothing here-below to trouble him. Finally, he gives the appearance of a harmonious concert, where the resonances and chords of the various faculties interweave, answer, and prolong one another, radiating the serene and opulent joy that one dreams of—that of belonging only to heaven.

In truth, peace is the hallowed ground where only the seeds planted by the Son can germinate. It is an atmosphere of delightful transparencies where only flowers of the Spirit may bloom. The man who knows how to acclimatize himself therein feels unexpectedly lighter. All that was pulling him downward finally breaks off, becomes detached from him little by little. His energies are being transformed. He mentally perceives new viewpoints. His heart thaws. His body changes in appearance, and his life force in quality. Finally, his whole person, detached from the natural focus of relative existence is grafted onto that of eternal life, the mystical vine. And when this transmutation is complete, the individual is forever fixed in God. He has become, to the letter, a child of heaven.

Such is the future reserved for those who, while pacifying their internal discord, try to put a stop to disputes and revenge. They need courage, because oftentimes both adversaries agree to fall upon them. They need a delicate sensitivity to be able to handle the wounds of conceit. They must have invincible meekness and benevolence, because all the malevolent gossip and unjust acts they will have prevented, inevitably fall back upon them. What constancy, love, and patience these peacemakers, according to God, must display! Let us admire, love, and humbly follow their rare example.

⊕

Blessed are they that are persecuted... The disciple's work does not consist only in maintaining or transforming the sinister ferments that are swarming within himself, even though that may be urgent. For apart from this, war must be waged also upon the ordinary outer evil of which men become the artisanal tools, and likewise upon the extraordinary outer evil by which devils reveal themselves. The first battle is the fight for justice; the second is the personal fight against temptations.

In his heart, the disciple has abandoned all that interests men. To them, he becomes a subject for scandal. They do not understand him. Outwardly, the closer they are to him the more surprised they are at his conduct. His former friends and family become the most hostile. They are not really to blame, because the light is not easy to capture: it likes to descend into inhospitable places. Disciples are often born into carnal families, where utilitarian covetousness reigns and religion is but a rote normality. Because on the part of the disciple there will be in this heavy atmosphere an energetic, direct effort toward heaven, the explosions for divine fervor will be that much more violent and pure, for the very presence of a disciple is an unbearable reproach to those who serve the powers of flesh and blood. The word "justice" connotes the idea of right; to render justice means restoring rights to those who have been deprived of them. To be just means, might I say, to act adroitly with rectitude in a rectilinear line of conduct. It means to possess a principle of conduct, and then allow oneself to think, love, or work only within the logic, within the radius, of this principle.

Men are always torn between two moral principles. The first, selfishness, has this sorry maxim: "Each man for himself and God for all." The second, altruism, has the sweet command: "Love ye one another." Hence, there are two kinds of right, and so two kinds of justice: the justice of matter is the law of retaliation; the justice of heaven is the vitality of love.

We associate the idea of combat with that of violence. We think of energy only in connection with the harshness of despotisms or in the rush of covetousness. But there are other battles and other extraordinary arms for the soldier of heaven. They are kindness, pity, patience, and indulgence. Outwardly, the soldier seems to be headed toward defeat: the world crushes him. Inwardly, the world becomes his stepping-stone; and since he combats on the side of eternity, his victory is assured.

Those legionnaires of divine folly are recruited from among the innovators, the martyrs of intellect, of idealism, or of faith; from among those that politics, laicism, or ecclesiasticism leave on the wayside to die—in order to glorify them later among the apostles of social fraternity or freedom of conscience. But Christ usually takes these faithful soldiers out from the anonymous crowd, from the streaming multitude among whom his penetrating eye discerns some souls old enough to have foresworn illusions, yet pure enough to see his splendor, and sufficiently malleable to accept total obedience. For them, the certitude of serving the Father is sufficient knowledge. They ask neither rest nor recompense. None of the marvels of the world fascinate them anymore. Their eyes are focused way beyond, upon the architect of marvels, upon the omniscient, upon the all-powerful who comes toward them as a friend, who gives them all he receives, and through whom they in turn can give their all to their weaker brothers.

These souls, no matter where they go, always carry their light—*the* light. In truth and verity, the kingdom of heaven belongs to them. Whether in radiant stars, in the depths of hells, or within the sorrowful solitudes where no stars have yet shone, heaven is theirs, since the Master of the heavens has made himself their servant.

Where does one really find a being who is constantly, totally, absolutely "persecuted for justice's sake"—one who is an innocent victim? If the victim is not innocent, then he is not a perfectly persecuted one. But no man, no matter what degree of sanctity he has obtained, is completely innocent—none but one alone, our Christ Jesus. His present promise, like those of the other seven beatitudes, as well as all of his promises, apply to himself. Moreover, as he sums up the kingdom of heaven, he gathers into one supreme unity the condition of his promise, its object, and the means of applying it to one's self. He is the one who promises, the promised one, and the one meriting the promise. Above all, he is the only poor, the only mourning, genially meek, hungry, merciful, pure, and persecuted one. He is, absolutely: proprietor of heaven, master of earth, consolation, justice, mercy, the vision of God, and the child of God. And all along evangelical history, this constant identity of teachings and acts, of promises and of their proofs, of the past with the future in the perpetual and mobile present—in short, the fusion of all that is abstract with all that is concrete—will be multiplied in the person of Jesus.

Yet, in order for the Christic force to affirm itself once more with the identification of extremes, we see an eternal, essential, and real happiness conferred as recompense for a misfortune that is merely temporary, since life on earth is so short; as recompense for a superficial misfortune, since only our personality can suffer; and as recompense for an apparent tragedy, since everything here-below is nothing but shadows and images. Such an infinite disproportion between temporal fate and eternal state exists for each of the beatitudes, although it is more visible in the eighth; it is the seal of the Son, the sending of hope.

⊕

The ninth beatitude. One sees hope, at the edge of the precipice, measuring in one glance the altitude of the skies before taking flight. In this glance are the two sentences where I want to find the ninth beatitude, the secret beatitude, the least known, the one everyone overlooks—just like the travelers of legends who failed to see the entrance to the treasure-cave hidden only by a fragile curtain of thorny bushes.

It is remarkable that St Luke, the most cultured of the apostles, mentions but three of the eight beatitudes, and even then only in the material sense. Was the historian of the long-suffering Mother of Christ more sensitive to physical suffering than were the other apostles, those strong men accustomed to hard labor? Or did he want to address himself to the lowest of the low, to the prisoners of the sad dungeon of uncelebrated wants.

In both hypotheses, the portraitist of the Virgin is right. Physical pain is a hard school, and our body a precious marvel. Whether we soften it or treat it as an enemy, we are still mistaken about it. Without our body, where would our soul be? What would our brain, our sensitivity, and all that makes us human be? Our admirable body is called to a dazzling role—shall it not become the temple of God? How prudently we should give it the exercises, labors, and that which elevates it to the Spirit; how we should respect it!

That is what I believe the third evangelist has wanted to make us understand, because in the deeper meaning he agrees with the first beatitude, since he describes in identical terms what I call the ninth beatitude—the synthesis of the preceding ones. (Luke 6:22–23)

These parallel verses show us clearly that Jesus was speaking, not to the crowd, but to his disciples, since, in order for the "persecuted ones to become blessed," they must have suffered because of him. This is how the secret of spiritual values is clearly revealed. These values are not to be found in energy, in grandeur, in how perfectly things were accomplished or borne, but in the motive, the aim, and intent that has been their basis. How often will Jesus refer to this arcanum!

Thus, if you who want to serve Jesus are outrageously treated, do not ask compensation; if people hate you, bow your head; if you are persecuted, do not defend yourself; if they slander you, do not try to make matters right by explaining facts. Each injury, each betrayal, each malicious act you have borne in your quality as disciple is one more certitude you have that someday you will sit at the right hand of God.

Here again, the kindly St Luke speaks with vengeance. He foretells woe upon the rich, upon those who have their fill, upon those who laugh, and upon those one speaks well of—and he is right. Those whom chance "spoils" become spoiled, alas! And the most difficult test to bear is luck, success, and wealth, rather than trials or poverty. That is why it is the duty of the wealthy to give, the duty of the scholar to teach, and the duty of the artist to nobly move others.

Hence, the law of matter is corruption, and the disciple who invokes the Spirit stops this corruption. It is thanks to this little group of true servants of heaven that corruption does not spread over the whole earth, and that this earth does not sink in one vertiginous fall into the bottomless abyss of nothingness. Just as sea water, when it evaporates, deposits as brilliant little crystals the pure substance that prevented it from putrefying, so when the heat of the divine Sun causes the material essences to evaporate from within us, we then have become nothing but fixity, solidity, purity; thus we check the morbid ferments.

These true disciples are not segregated, neither do they constitute a religious sect. The Spirit that animates and sustains them needs no label. Do not believe that you will find them as a congregation of cloistered monks, or in some unknown ashram, or as a part of any mysterious fraternity. They may be found here and there, but their cloister is the Spirit. They themselves probably do not know what they are, whereas Lao-Tze, Gautama, Caesar, and Napoleon knew who they were. By that fact, they were small in the eyes of God. The Virgin, sole representative of the assembly of the workers of God, had no opinion of herself save that she felt unworthy and lowly.

The very fact that the true disciples ignore their status makes them the salt and the lamp: were they to use part of their energy to worry about themselves, they would work less and radiate less.

To understand who Jesus Christ is, to feel that no career is better than the one of entering into his service, and to try to follow his path, means that we have before our birth been chosen for the secret cohort of his disciples. We must do our utmost to remain pure and lily-white; we must constantly hold aloft the lamp we have received. All of our thoughts should be subject to the law, all of our desires focused upon heaven, all of our gestures prolongations of the gestures of Christ. We must offer our sympathy to everything, and to everyone say what we believe to be true. Remember that Jesus is here, and, finally, to offer and entrust ourselves to him often.

Salt represents inner purity. The lamp represents the gift of all we possess, or better still, the gift of one's self. Doubtless, we must give alms, give out our discoveries, share our knowledge, and offer our happiness; but with all this, we must still include the smile of fraternal friendship. Let us imitate the Father, who distributes to all beings—no matter what their quality—the life, food, and intelligence needed for their progress, and who does not know how to refuse them anything, but for the inopportune favors they would use for wrongdoing. In short, salt does not mean to believe one's self to be pure, but to be pure; because, the purpose of salt is not to remain in a beautiful crystal container, but to be incorporated in the foods that are ever ready to spoil. It does not mean to speak well of God, but to act in accord with him. The act alone is an illuminating light.

Before proceeding further with the Sermon on the Mount, let us throw a last look upon those tremendous first words. We know pleasure, contentment, enchantment, felicity, ravishment, and ecstasy: these are the human expressions of joy. And the divine expression of joy is beatitude: a state wherein motion is a pleasure, where vigor is reborn even as it spends itself, where fatigue does not exist anymore, where one finds the answer as soon as one begins to search, where one receives the moment one asks, where possession fills a desire without ever satisfying it. This is beatitude.

None can visualize it. Our joys are its shadows, just as the sun is the shadow of the light. Any created thing is a limit, a negation, and a hollow. Our joys are but the illusory possessions of these appearances. Our beatitudes will be the true joy of eternal realities that fall upon our souls and possess them forever.

What can one say, when the mouth of Jesus has uttered a word? Eight times he has repeated: "Blessed are...," and the ninth time, to summarize the first eight. Why, if not to make us understand that happiness awaits us, and that we will be happy in that destiny. The most scholarly of his priests have taught our ancestors that faith comes from the Father and charity from the Spirit, but that hope belongs to the Son. Hope is the state of appeal, the force of desire, the daughter of faith, and the mother of charity.

The doctors of the Church teach us that in the divine work of salvation each of the three persons of the Trinity helps us through a special force. The help from the Father is faith, that from the Spirit is charity, and that from the Son is hope. Now, there is a "human" faith called will, a "normal" charity called philanthropy, and a hope "within reason" called optimism. But the eternal forces that are rebuilding within us this all-virginal heart (the only heart able to have a vision of God) are, by contrast to those just mentioned, "super" human, "beyond" our normal state, and "abnormal" to our reason. So must they be, because they descend from the absolute in order to reascend, taking us along with them.

Thus, the whole mission of the Son is but a universal

sowing of limitless hope. In fact, he did not save us. He only brought us the means of salvation: the world was in such a state that without him, salvation was impossible. It is up to us to put these means to work. He guides us to the bridge that is himself. And when, through our own good-will, we have reached it, he makes us to cross the chasm. But his first public discourse—woven with hope, his miracles, his parables, his precepts, his actions, his ever new timelessness—is still but a vast picture of living hope. He humanizes God. He brings infinite heaven within our reach. He brings mysteries within our understanding. He shows us the little flowers of our fields, and hearts as faraway distant daughters of the eternal hills and of the smiles of angels.

We are well aware that Christ brings us faith with charity, since he brings us, in the flesh, God, total and supreme—and since his works are certitude and tenderness. But the special gift he offers us, the true gift that sustains and is hidden beneath all others, is hope. Without hope, how could we believe in the ineffable, why would we love the indifferent? Hope always goes forward. It dashes toward the future, untiring, inextinguishable. Faith sometimes leans upon miracles, as does charity sometimes upon palpable sorrows. But hope leans upon that which does not yet exist, and feeds upon very faraway dreams.

Hope is the first operation of this meagre exchange that God holds with men. Jesus brings to them the flower, perfume, and elixirs known as very precious hope; and in payment, he accepts their meager and pale hopes. Repentance alone transmutes these anemic wishes into powerful flights through and beyond the worlds, up even to the throne of the Father.

Thus, this discourse of the beatitudes, the first words spoken by the Word to men, urges them to the impossible, chases them away from worldly promises, and, finally, quickens within them the inestimable nostalgia for heaven.

Now comes the order of this adventurous exploration.

The New Law

O NOT think that I have come to set aside the law and the prophets; I have not come to set them aside, but to bring them to perfection. Believe me, till heaven and earth pass, one iota or one flourish shall in no wise disappear from the law; it must all be accomplished. Heaven and earth will pass away, but my words will not. Whoever, then breaks one of these commandments, though it were the least and teaches men to do likewise, will be of least account in the kingdom of heaven; but the man who keeps them and teaches others to keep them will be called great in the kingdom of heaven.

And I tell you, that if your justice does not surpass the justice of the scribes and pharisees, you shall not enter into the kingdom of heaven.

You have heard that it was said to the men of old: Thou shalt not murder; if a man commits murder, he must answer for it before the court of justice. But I tell you that any man who gets angry at his brother must face judgment, and he who says "Raca" (worthless empty-headed man) to his brother must answer for it before the council; and any man who says: "Thou fool" must answer for it in hell fire.

If, when bringing thy gift before the altar, thou rememberest that thy brother has some ground of complaint against thee, then leave thy gift lying there before the altar; go and be reconciled with thy brother first, and then come back to offer thy gift.

If any man has a claim against thee, come to terms then and there, while thou art walking in the road with him, for fear the claimant may hand thee over to the judge, and the judge to the officer, and that thou wilt be cast into prison. Believe me, thou shalt not be set at liberty until thou hast paid the last farthing.

You have heard that it was said: Thou shalt not commit adultery. But I tell you that he who casts his eyes on a woman so as to lust after her has already committed adultery with her in his heart.

If thy right eye is the occasion of thy falling into sin, pluck it out and cast it away from thee; better to lose one part of thy body than to have the whole cast into Gehenna. And if thy right hand is an occasion of falling, cut if off and cast it away from thee; better to lose one of thy limbs than to have the whole body fall into Gehenna.

It was said, too, Whoever will put away his wife must first give her a writ of separation. But I tell thee the man who puts away his wife (setting aside the matter of unfaithfulness) makes an adulteress of her, and whoever marries her after she has been put away commits adultery.

You have heard also that it was said to the men of old, Thou shalt not perjure thyself; thou shalt perform what thou hast sworn in the sight of the Lord. But I tell you that you should not bind yourselves by any oath at all: not by heaven, for heaven is God's throne; nor by earth, for earth is the footstool under his feet; nor by Jerusalem, for it is the city of the great king. And thou shalt not swear by thy own head, for thou hast no power to turn a single hair of it white or black. Let your word be yes for yes, and no for no; whatever goes beyond this comes from the evil one.

You have heard that it was said, An eye for an eye and a tooth for a tooth. But I tell you that you should not offer resistance to injury; if a man strikes thee on thy right cheek, turn the other cheek also toward him; if he is ready to go to the law with thee over thy coat, let him have it and thy cloak with it; if he compels thee to attend him on a mile journey, go two miles with him of thy own accord.

Give to him who asks, and if a man would borrow from thee, do not turn away; and whoever takes what belongs to you, do not reclaim it.

You have heard that it was said, Thou shalt love thy neighbor and hate thy enemy. But I tell you: Love your enemies, do good to those who hate you, speak with kindness of those who damn you; pray for those who persecute and insult you, so that you may be true sons of your Father in heaven, who makes his sun rise equally on the evil ones and on the good, and his rain fall on the just as on the unjust.

If you love those who love you, what title have you to a reward? Do not the publicans do as much? If you greet none but your brethren, what more are you doing than others? Do not the heathens do as much? And if you

> only do good to those who treat you well, what thanks can you expect? Even sinners love those who love them. What credit is it to you if you lend to those from whom you expect repayment? Even sinners lend to sinners, to receive as much in exchange.
>
> Be merciful as your Father is merciful...
> Be perfect as your Father is perfect...[1]

The Father is One in his essence. The innumerable manifestations of his will are one; his infinitely complex connections are one with all that exists. His unity contains all that which is possible, as well as the impossible. The pinnacle toward which he launches all creatures is himself; their original point of departure was himself. He is simultaneous, indivisible, permanent. Yet, our words can only convey the idea of a synthetic reconstitution; while there are none to portray his living, spontaneous, and concrete Oneness.

The sages whose minds soar from one abstraction to another—on to the concept of a principle—conceive and describe the Father by negations: the *ab*solute, the *im*movable, the *in*finite, the *im*mobile. He *is* all that—when viewed from the angle of creation. But God's friends, his followers who live in him and contemplate him with the eyes of love, see him as spontaneous motion and permanent affirmation. He is the sum-total of all our visions, even beyond what our vastest imagination could conceive.

Thus, the Father never repents, he never readjusts his designs, or betters his plans, which are perfect from the principle. The changes he seems to bring to his works are in

[1] Matthew 5:17–48; Mark 11:25, 10:11; Luke 16:17, 21:33, 12:58–59, 16:18, 6:27, 36.

reality new facts that he draws from the bottomless treasure of his love, in order that they may serve as crutches for the floundering free-will of creatures. The differences existing between moral laws only represent opportunisms adapted to the differences of needs, of epochs, and of psychological resources.

According to the quality of their spiritual work, people receive new rules, the observance of which brings them to a higher or lower rank. This same condition holds true for the earth, the universe, even for future universes still gestating in the limbo of possibility.

It has been said that the philosophy of Christ was not new. It is true that one finds similar maxims in Taoist teachings, in the Brahmanic slokas, in Buddhist sutras, in Celtic triads, in the Talmud, the Koran, and in the book of the Bab. But these are merely similarities of form: the essence differs. A skillful hypnotist, for instance, can induce phenomena of ecstasy or clairvoyance in a subject which to the casual observer seem identical to those experienced by a saint. Yet their causes are complete opposites. The impartial observer quickly perceives the radical differences likewise: for them, Christ could only repeat what the great religious initiates had already said in substance. Would it be admissible for the Father to have left such multitudes in error and ignorance since the beginning of time? So, Christ came, not so much to teach through words as to demonstrate through deeds. He showed us the way through the power of his total, immortal example. "He came not to obey, but to fulfill"; that which he brought is new hope based upon experiential proofs. The law remains whole, integral. It is only susceptible of modifications and developments as measured by what we have accomplished according to our comprehension of it. And as actual events prove, we are far from that state of accomplishment. Let us not be surprised that we have to meet the same problems time and time again. Such as it is, the code of spiritual ethics contains work for many centuries still to come.

This is a great undertaking, of course, but an excellent, lofty, and mighty one. It is the very work itself; the true reason for the world. Never will we understand it sufficiently! It is for us that the Father has built this world. He gave it to us. It is ours. Its fate rests in our hands—not only its amelioration, but its temporal duration. Divine law gives us indications of how we should treat this universe, rather like a professor who, once having given a problem to his students, makes them work on it until they have the correct answer. The smallest accent of the law will remain till we have inscribed and sculpted it into the material substance of the worlds to which we are sent—because the law is God's Will, and the Will of God is his Word Jesus.

Jesus shoulders the work of the preceding founders of religions. He consolidates, renews, and rejuvenates it. He adds to it an undisclosed light. He vivifies that work by breathing his own life into it. Finally, he brings it to that degree of relative perfection to which the spiritual state of the earth is susceptible. We should collaborate toward this accomplishment. Although the Father promulgates this law only for creatures—yet, because he pronounces it, he gives it an eternal essence. Though heaven and earth may pass away, the law not only remains intact but will remain after everything that was the particular cause of its proliferation has been reintegrated into its place of origin: the kingdom of heaven. At that moment, this law, finding its primal splendor again, will also return to its origin: the Word of the Father. It will rest in him and be indescribably magnified with all the virtues creatures will have added to it while bringing it to fruition during these universal cycles.

The Law, the Word, the Will of the Father totally realized, the maturity of the World, the perfect development of beings, the resurrection of the flesh—are all synonymous terms. On this account, it is very simple to conceive that our passage down-here is but the means for our perpetual presence above, for obedience to the law gives us an infallible right to a place in the eternal world, from which this law is but a transitory refraction broken into components

In order to find a reason for life, we must recognize that what man's pride calls, with rancor, "divine good-pleasure" really means: "things are thus because God wants them so." Any philosophy that does not admit an independent primordial cause breaks on the reefs of pessimism, inaction, and revolt. God launched us into time and space so that during this long voyage a certain force—of which we do not know the true nature, but think of as living knowledge—may increase in us. Whether we will or no, we have to take that voyage. Our resistance only causes it to last longer, so our most expedient method is to undertake it freely with good will.

Whatever might be the philosophy our intellect adopts, the solution I am indicating to you is the one that lessens our sufferings, worries, and sorrows, and that elevates us to the highest possible pinnacles of serene energy and judicious wisdom. Let us not forget that the Father decrees in the absolute, but his decisions reach the various worlds at successive moments in duration. In God, in his kingdom, everything is the present—simultaneous, ceaselessly reborn with increasing power—whereas in nature the present is a mobile mathematical point where everything wears away without recourse. But this point of the present, this small aperture open upon the eternal, this "invariable middle" of which the Chinese sages speak, is the ever-flowing spark, which the Word sows among us throughout centuries, whose ardor and splendor he measures according to the luminous capacity of the beings who will have to encounter it. Thus, God communicates his creative plans to man through the law that he inscribes within our conscience, and he illustrates this spiritual text by showing us, through his Son Jesus, the realization, the materialization, and the fulfillment of this law.

The law of Moses was merely an extract from the law of the Father, for use by the Israelites. It was not on that account a deformation: it was holy and divine and perfect for the purpose for which the Theocrat imposed it. The Father directs a nebula, a planet, or a man in the same manner, because any creature is his child. He furnishes each of them with a certain allowance of intelligences and vitalities that they must put to work. These latter then choose through their own free will their mode of work, whether it be selfish or altruistic, because only work done willingly has any eternal value. Throughout these long ages, God manifests himself to his children only under such guise as intuitions of moral conscience, or through partial teachings to the most advanced ones. However, if a creature, no matter who it be, strays so far that none of its elder brothers can bring it any help, the Father himself descends to its aid. And this descent is the Son, the Messiah, Christ: our Jesus.

Without Jesus, there is no road between the relative and the absolute. The world floats upon the abyss of nothingness, between the nights of hells and the suns of paradises.

But as soon as the Word incarnates upon a planet, a path is opened from that place up to the House of the Father, and men can take that path by following the orders of the Word, and thereby draw along all other creatures in their wake. Let us note that this direct route between each man and God is ever new. The traveler walks through unknown territory, and so must maintain a strong grip on the only certain guide: Christ.

Even the most profound sages have never been able to see but the secondary goals of the providential design—as for example, our future happiness. The design itself remains ever unknowable. Never does a general of generals communicate his plans to his soldiers.

A king, having adjudged that the economic or civil standards of his subjects would be raised if directed in some particular manner, promulgates legislation to this end. So the Father, when considering the goal for which he has created us, furnishes us with the resources, tells us which activities, among others, we are to pursue in order to reach that goal whose unknownness is a given condition of our work. Only divine laws are perfect and conceived for our own advantage. They lead us to the ideal stasis of our development by the shortest road. They coincide with all the mutual relationships among all creatures. They are the schema of the universe and the formulae of its life.

That is why our disobedience or revolts delay the march of the world and foment death therein. That is why we suffer. For any ordeal is but a personal experience of an evil that our immortal will has previously called into existence owing to an infraction of the law.

But let us stop developing this theme. The ensemble of the designs of the Father is written in a book sealed to any creature. It is called the Book of Life. The Mosaic law is no more than a terrestrial echo of one of the letters from this book. The *Law of Manu*, the *I Ching*, the *Avesta*, were other echoes of the various divine letters. Our duty does not lie in groping researches or in hazardous attempts to reconstruct this spiritual text, but in the simple realization of the minimal part that has been revealed to us. The New Testament, the conscience, and the exhortations of God's servants down through the centuries tell us what our duties are. And when we have executed one of them perfectly, the next—a little more difficult—is taught to us according to our strength and to the milieu wherein we are living. At intervals we do meet minds to whom each letter and each accent of the sacred text is clearly intelligible. But this is a gift, a privilege that becomes warped if violated. The best method of acquiring a healthy and a true religious science is to limit our efforts to the fulfillment of our duty: everything else is but pride and puerility.

Not a tittle of the law will be erased before it has been realized throughout the universe. Do you know that it might be you yourself whom heaven awaits, in order to terminate the incarnation of a particular letter or a particular comma of the eternal text? Hence, let us devote ourselves wholeheartedly to the smallest chores, and never leave them except when completed and done well.

The collaboration to which Jesus invites us is in any case a difficult and entirely new enterprise. The ancient sacred books did not contain everything. Lao Tze, Vyasa, and Zoroaster themselves give us to understand that they do not know everything. Among the Kabbalists, those who have acknowledged the Messiah say that the *Song of Songs* was sung only by one half of the choir from the tribe of

Levi, and that the second half sang it only after the coming of Christ. Irenaeus Agnostus, Fludd, and Madathanus, who in the seventeenth century attempted to merge polytheistic initiation with Christian revelation under the locution of the Rose-Croix, have pointed out the alternations of the seventy-two singers. But—please permit me to affirm this to you—these men, scholarly and wise, whose writings contain, for whoever wants to delve deeply into them, so many ingenious sparks, still have not perceived the limitlessness of the evangelical horizons. I do not scorn any of these adepts, and I know that the doctrines they taught were excellent for their respective peoples. But heed this divine counsel: "Let the dead bury the dead and go toward life." For the past two thousand years, Solomon could not have stated nor repeated: "There is nothing new under the sun." There *is* something new, an ever-renewed newness that revivifies itself ceaselessly.

Go to this infinitely flowing freshness. Go to Jesus. Each day you will discover in him another unknown beauty; each day he will open a secret door within you and lead you into hitherto unknown gardens.

By the very fact that they live, even the lowest among beings influence all others. This radiation is their own word. Among all beings, man has received the greatest verbal power; but having used it badly for a long time, he has weakened it to such a degree that his acts radiate more than his words upon earth today.

On the other hand, we all have the tendency of making our neighbors work, rather than working ourselves. Our neighbor's duty seems more important than ours. As to our own duties, it happens that we do not even wish to see them. (Matthew 5:20) This is the state of mind Jesus calls "the justice of scribes and pharisees." The law of the created world is that any action calls for a reaction. This holds true in the intelligible plane as well as in the feeling plane; in the plane of passion as well as in the world of wills. Nature is a sphere poised between the abyss from above and the abyss from below; selfishness pulls it to the depths while altruism pushes it heavenward. As to acts that might be neither good nor bad, they do not exist, though certain species of metaphysics consider such indifference to be the very perfection of the created being and its liberation. This pseudo-serenity of reason—this "intellectual" wisdom—whether clothed in Buddhist, Gnostic, or Quietist terms, is the very one that Jesus qualified as pharisaic, and that he asks us to surpass. For the world to be saved, disciples must hurl it heavenward, toward the disequilibrium of love.

If we wish to enter heaven someday, we must from this moment on create heaven on earth. For us to receive later on the infinite plenitude of science, wisdom, and power, we must from this moment on give to others all we possess. We must surpass our normal tasks. If we become the servants of our brothers now, the angels will serve us in heaven after our judgment.

Here is another way of "surpassing the justice of the scribes": by trying to spare others the whiplash of their past or present mistakes, by preventing them from hurting themselves, by luring the drunkard away from the bar, and the miser from his safe—and to do it in such a way that they are not even aware of our fraternal ruse, so that if they do return to their vice, they are not angry at us, and therefore do not have to shoulder a dual responsibility.

But these ameliorations are not obtainable without a great deal of meekness and patience, without suppling our mentality, character, and temperament. The lintel of heaven's door is very low, and one must become so very small in order to pass beneath it. In that way, through indulgence and fraternal kindness, let us call down all the love the Father eagerly awaits to give us, so that mercy may surpass justice and that the New Covenant will reign over a reborn earth.

Let us follow our Master in minute, practical, applications: first, against murder, adultery, swearing, and vengeance; then, finally, comes the positive precept: love for our brother.

⊕

Murder. It is written: Thou shalt not kill. The context clearly indicates that here one is faced with individual, man-to-man murders. To allege that Christ thereby means to forbid soldiers to kill the enemies of their country is to take liberties with the precept. The absolute pacifists confine one term of their syllogism in the absolute and the other in the relative: their logic errs.

International war could not exist if, within each nation, men were brotherly. Everywhere, in provinces, cities, hamlets, and families, we attack and hurt one another in all manner of ways. These jealousies and ruses, these local and personal spites, fatally draw the warrior demons. What a utopia it is to believe that peace might reign among peoples, when there is so much hatred from house to house.

On the other hand, the soldier does not defend himself; he defends the totality of his compatriots. He defends the body and soul of his country. Even when he dies for her, he only returns to her what he received from her at birth. Also: where is the pacifist who will throw himself between two enemy troops to stop them in the name of a higher principle at the risk of being killed?

Since we claim that divine law forbids any kind of murder, how then are we going to keep alive? Each breath kills thousands of little living beings in our body and in the atmosphere. When we dress in the morning we also kill innumerable cells. Vegetarian idealists are against the killing of animals, yet a plant lives just as intense a life as does the sheep. We cannot experience a sensation, register a fact in our brain, elaborate a thought, or even extend our hand, without killing some cells.

That is not the point. We must accept life as at is, and it is we ourselves who have opened to death the door of life. Each expression of anger, contempt, selfishness, or larceny is an additional force given to the power of destruction. Let us accept our load. If our body needs flesh foods, let the body have them, but we must learn how to conquer the instinctive reactions that this diet provokes. If our country needs to be defended, let us fearlessly fulfill our soldierly duty, without cruelty or anger.

Also, we fail to remember prayer. Ancient religions were concerned with the fate of the animals whose flesh we eat. The rites that accompanied the sacrifices took away from the spirit of the victim most of its suffering. Each Christian can do the same by asking the sole innocent Victim—the mystical Lamb—to lessen the agony of these lower beings, and also to lessen the debt contracted by man toward them, by considering that man will use strength, revitalized at their expense, for service to his brothers. That is the purpose served by the *Benedicite* hymn of the Christians.

Each of our actions should in any event surely be preceded by a similar request that heaven remove any evil that could enter into it. Also, each day God grants us should begin with the words "Thy will be done" as well as by the "Deliver us from evil" of the Lord's Prayer.

Moses forbade corporal murders only. Jesus forbids also the spiritual murders that are impatience, scorn, and anger—even toward animals and things. Everything has intelligence and sensibility. Your hand that strikes, whether a horse or a piece of furniture, instills furor equally within them: the beast can become nasty, the table can communicate the obscure influence of irritation to whoever is seated there after you. Man is such a center of live influences that he involuntarily sanctifies or renders evil everything he touches, even everything he looks at.

Anger has to be answered for by a court of judgment (Matthew 5:22) because it obliges the angry man to find himself later in the same position as the one his is oppressing, and also to undergo the violence of another angry man. And thus it goes on and on until one of these irascibles is able to control his bad humor. The insult we throw in the face of someone, even if it seems merited, drags us at death invisibly before a pitiless tribunal. To call someone crazy with the intent of offending them makes us run the risk of experiencing someday the consuming anguish known as insanity.

Anger, scorn, abuse, come from the heart, hence we must appease, soften, tame, and finally sublimate them.

⊕

What process shall we follow, since it is written: Thou shalt not kill? Anger is an energy from darkness that has to be transmuted into an energy of light. Just as overcoming obesity is obtained, not by fasting, but by physical exercise, we must cure our irritable nature by employing its force to forgive. Whoever has undertaken that task knows what a veritable "moral backache" one has to endure. That is why Jesus speaks of forgiveness.

Please note that Jesus asks of us to follow this severe training just at the most necessary times: whenever we appeal to divine justice through prayers, or appeal to human justice through legal proceedings. Any prayer, no matter how feeble, partial, superficial, or even artificial we suppose it to be, is a reaching out of ourselves toward the ideal of equilibrium, of peace, and of harmony. If the spiritual part of man ascends toward this serenity while in a state of furor, it will bounce back, and his furor will be increased. He will have added fuel to the fire, and after terminating his prayer will be worse off than when he began his ascent.

But this is a general statement. Whenever we speak to God, should we not first of all stop conversing with other people—which means, should we not momentarily forget even our worries, desires, impatience, and rancors? Such a state of forgetting is reached first by placing our entire confidence in the Father, then resigning ourselves to his will, since he asks nothing more from us than to do our utmost. Then we must forgive the offenses we think we have borne—and forgive instantly, because of the process it follows. Let me try to describe it.

No action—and, in this case, no insult or injury—is viable in itself. It lives only through the feeling that produced it. This feeling is an act in the central realm of the Word, from where our heart, our animic center, originated. The guides, guardians, and angels with which the Word surrounds us know us by feeling. They see neither our corporeal form nor our mental form. It is the heart they see. They perceive its humiliations, its rancors, its feelings of vengeance and of forgiveness. Peace must then be consummated between the same four parties of a quarrel: the two adversaries and their two angels. And these four are probably together only today, at the most, during this particular lifetime. Who knows where, after death, they will meet in the purgatory of Catholicism, or in the numerous worlds of the reincarnationists? And when? The safest course is to be reconciled right away, rather than drag for several cycles the vampirish load of an anger or a grudge. (Matthew 5:23–24)

Immediate forgiveness is but one example of the rule that commands never to postpone till the morrow what can be done today. Nothing ever comes isolated: men, happenings, circumstances, are veritable little worlds. Groups meet groups, which each of us represents, in the presence of other groups, which are spectators. At the moment when a certain test is given us, the auxiliary or inspirational forces necessary for this task to be accomplished as best can be are there also. And if we postpone this task, these forces will be gone tomorrow, because everything evolves and revolves from a certain standpoint. In this, everything resembles a planetary system. Thus, the faithful disciple must be able to command himself instantaneously, so as never to refuse making an effort.

Also, many things we believe important, really are not so. Let us beware of our judgment. Also, please note that Christ mentions the quarrelers and he orders them to be reconciled, but nowhere does he mention that we have to determine who was right or wrong. In a quarrel there is doubtless an offender and an offended one, but as I have often observed, generally both parties believe they are the offended ones. Alas! if our gravest personal debates seem rather puerile to the philosopher, how much more childish they must seem to an intelligence anchored in God! The desire expressed by Christ is that we abstain from quarrels and lawsuits, even when they seem merely to be defensive; it is an excellent school for shrinking the self and bringing it down from its pedestal.

Let us follow this school during life, while on the path; because, at the end, a Judge is awaiting us. There is not a worry which comes our way that we have not brought forth: perhaps an hour ago; perhaps centuries ago; maybe in this very room; maybe in some world imperceptible to the telescope. Let us adopt the habit, in superficial little circumstances, never to contest, dispute, or acrimoniously criticize. Yes, in the esthetic, intellectual, and scientific domains, we must and should be able to evaluate. But comparison is not condemnation. And an artist who creates a masterpiece, a thinker who offers us a wholesome doctrine, a scientist who explains life, and an accomplisher of deeds who attenuates social suffering, are doing more for the progress of humanity than are all the critics, the envious, the polemicists, and the politicians. True progress is not destructive, but constructive.

The invisible tribunal is equitable. It judges passionlessly and follows a precise code. Spiritual penalties never exceed our culpabilities. Physiological taints, castigations of destiny, intellectual deficiencies, and moral shortcomings are the chains and walls of the dungeon. It is we who have laid up the ones and forged the others. We are the prisoners of our own selves, and we will remain captive as long as we have not furnished the experimental proof to the ministers of destiny that we can put our liberty to good use. We will be truly free one day, but we must cultivate the precious seeds. This cultivation means obliging the self to obey Christ; for is not doing what we want, doing what pleases us? If we have already lived before, are not our tastes the fruits of prenatal covetousness? And, if this life should be the only one we were to experience, are not our tastes the very obstacles God wants our soul to overcome? Are they not the defects he gives it to combat? Thus, we will not leave this dungeon before having worn the irons down, or demolished the walls, before having paid all the debts that selfishness shouldered us with, while it satisfied its wants at the expense of other beings. If we apply the strict eye-for-an-eye law of talion to others, destiny will inflict the same law upon us. But if we remit and forgive, heaven will indemnify destiny in our place and calm the indignation of our victims. Only then will we be free, will we be able to leave the world of incarnations, of matter, of the relative, and of the temporal—in order to enter into the world of the spirit, into the absolute, into the eternal.

⊕

Marriage and family. After the rules that regulate social relationships, here is the rule regarding marriage, the principle of the family. (Matthew 5:27–32)

All the ancient religions enjoin physical fidelity. The choice made by two fiancés is only apparently free. In the majority of cases, destiny had a hand in it. Certain parents may only have certain children. This is because heredity is not just physiological, nor an atavism, nor social only: married couples, parents, and children have a correspondence that follows the unknown laws of spiritual necessities. The most fructifying marriages for the souls are not always, and rarely are, the happiest in the human sense.

Polygamy, useful to races physically new, is an opportunism, just as the license for divorce was in the Mosaic law, about which Jesus will be questioned later. Monogamy alone permits human love to emerge out of carnal passion, then out of sentimental passion, in order to land upon "the happy shores" where fraternal, pure, and silent tenderness surpasses the sublimest heights of sentimentalism and romanticism and gives a few predestined couples, happy in their reciprocal sacrifice, the presentiment of the serene beatitudes of eternal love.

Seen from the heights of the spirit, marriage is a very elementary school. Seen from our level, however, it constitutes a work worthy of all our diligence, because it offers the best occasions of attaining perfect control of the will over the habitual gestures of selfishness, over the manias we wallow in, over our paltry oddities, over easy and banal opinions, over that ensemble of hypocrisy and self-delusions that too often make our life, from our maturity on, so apathetic, inconsequential, narrow, ugly, and rigidified. A husband and wife who until death would have belonged to each other totally, whose every thought, tastes, and sensations would have been spontaneous exchanges, who as spouses would have lived but for each other without a single distraction, would have attained a clarity, an integrity, an inner transparency that would prepare them for the most marvelous adventures on the road to heaven.

The human being offers the excellent example of a whole formed out of the most disparate parts, cemented by invincible cohesion. The fugitive contact between a finger and an object not only provokes physical, chemical, magnetic, and electrical reactions, but it also acts on the imponderable organisms that psychology believes to be formless forces. It also acts upon the farthest clouds within the obscure heavens of the unconscious. Inversely, the wake of the flight of an angel way beyond Sirius, the gesture of a creature upon Neptune, always reach some receptive post in the very depths of the self and provoke even in our entrails and upon our epidermis modifications that could be registered in a laboratory by instruments sufficiently sensitive. These are the general facts, the particular applications of which render comprehensible the various and still unknown reasons for the moral dictates promulgated by the gospel.

Our five senses are doors wide open to temptations. The least extra-conjugal desire is a theft prejudicial to the other spouse and an outrage to the integrity of the person to whom it is directed: that which constitutes the sin is the inner willingness, even when it is not followed by the fulfillment owing to many circumstances that might place obstacles in the way. Let us remember that our acts always engender multiple effects and that our desires terminate in multiple deceits. Let us acquire a deeper respect for the liberty of others and a more profound feeling for the importance of our own promises. In spite of ourselves, we are bound by our word in the world of causes. But in the world of effects, particularly on this earth, let us be voluntary slaves. The entire integral culture of an individual rests upon this double and mutual relationship between the physical and the psychic. It is not sufficient to think well. We must act well. It is not sufficient to act well. We must think well. The great educators have stressed the control of ideas, of feeling, and of imagination as the most important part of their method. In fact, the subtlest dominates the most dense. An act may be good and its thought evil; but if the intention, the thought, and the will are just, loyal, and pure, the act will always be good, regardless of the possible errors in the adjusting. That is why religious asceticism orders the daily practice of meditation: once, twice, three times a day, the disciple faces himself, examines himself as if he were divided in two. He interrogates himself, compares his desires and his acts to the divine model, then self-imposes reparations, and decrees the resolutions he must follow. No other system procures a better psychic mastery; and it is this continuous habit, whose influence radiates little by little upon the profane and temporal objects of their acts, which gives to many monks and priests their authority over laic conscience, gives depth to their purpose, and constancy in their realizations.

But here I must draw the independent searcher's and the unattached spiritual-minded man's attention to a snare. These people may be, and are, positive about the primordial importance of what the gospel calls "purification of the heart," of this patient cultivation that lops from our desires and decisions any and all elements of cupidity, enjoyment, or personal benefit. But they may be, and often are, tempted to have recourse, with that end in view, to the more or less wise but always illicit practices of the Eastern temples: breathing exercises; mental concentration by means of the immobility of the eyes, special postures, special diets, drugs, subjective meditations, contemplations, and ecstasies by means of magneto-telluric currents, etc., etc.

A whole literature—first English, then American, then German, French, and Russian—has been vulgarizing these artifices through the Western world for the past forty years or so. But in Asia, where the atmosphere seconds the climate, the mental attitude, the social customs, nutrition, and physiological heredity join together in offering the experimenter all sorts of facilities; and yet, according to the statement of the authoritative adepts, there are but four or five successful results among thousands of tryouts. In Europe, where everything stands opposed to this type of introspection, should we not expect pathological and psychological catastrophes to happen among the foolhardy students?

There is no better process to conquer oneself than the tenacious, incessant, untiring struggle against one's selfish tendencies. Each morning we should note precisely the point upon which we failed the previous day, and never, no matter at what cost, deviate one iota from our course during the whole day. The smallest detail is important: a sentence, an angrily spoken word, shaking a finger, an eyelid that involuntarily twitches—are all to be mastered. The one minute of relaxation we may grant ourselves because of laziness will be the cause a little later during the day when at work, or in the evening when at prayers, of a long and disconcerting distraction. A great fault is always the daughter of a little forgetfulness. Each negligence digs into us a perfidious vampiric mouth where later our efforts toward order, organization, and clarity will be invincibly engulfed. No other course of life, whatever be its social spheres, demands more reason, more precise will-power and energy, than does the life of the disciple. To recognize one's duty in a simple and sincere glance, and then to accomplish it, no matter how painful or insignificant in appears: that is the rule. (Matthew 5:29–30)

The finest tactic in overcoming temptation is not to

become exalted, gesticulating in tumultuous gyrations, but on the contrary to remain still, calm, unobtrusive, very small. You have often observed men who became agitated, who gesticulated while shouting: "No, I won't do that..." who, after a few clever maneuvers of his opponent, finally acquiesced to his demand; while another man who says "No" in a quiet voice, can never be made to change his mind to "Yes." As the Tempter will always be more crafty, more cunning than we—violence and ruse being his domain—therefore, stillness and calm disarm him.

Also, temptation is not mere psychology. Everything in man is connected. Any perception may later become a thought. Any thought ends by modifying the body. It is not only our spirit that is tempted, but also all of its rays: the spirit of our ears, eyes, and fingers. If one of these organs does evil, it is because its animating principle has lost its way in the land of evil—and cells travel in our body just as the stars move in the firmament. A morbid germ that has been brought into the body by the divagations of a vital spirit can then infect successively the whole psychic person. And if, for example, we permit the intelligence of our hand to steal or brutalize, then, when some of the cells—still some forces of that hand—will have reached the brain, our thought will become murderous or thievish, and our will will be unable to resist it.

If at a grave period of our psychic life the temptation of murder visits us, then, rather than commit a murder, it would be preferable for us to follow the gospel to the letter and cut off this definitely corrupt hand. Even though my body does not belong to me, even though by mutilating myself, I commit an "abuse of power," the evil will be less incurable (because partial) than the more complete evil I would have engendered if I had obeyed the impulse to kill. (Matthew 5:30)

Hell, like heaven, is everywhere. Its purifying pangs reach us no matter where we live. It is impossible to escape payments due, even were we to exercise upon our organs the pitiless discipline that Christ speaks of here in the hope of being saved, or for fear of a spiritually difficult future. We would only swap one pain for another. We would not be preparing our salvation. But if we are impelled to the fanatical extremity of a mutilation (which so shocks modern delicacy) because we are overwhelmed by repentance, the Father will annul the results of this violent remedy and still welcome us to his side.

As disconcerting and barbarous as these ideas may seem to you, do not cast them aside at first sight. Look at the frightful fecundity of a wrong action. Begin counting its offshoots in the social order, in the intellectual order, in families, in physiology, as well as within the invisible worlds. A sin does not corrupt the sinner only. Every moment we come in contact with hundreds of forces and beings that we either purify or pervert. Look also at the universe of love, which dwells beyond human reason and plain justice, and you will see that these remedies which ordinary Christians only see as rhetorical figures are one of the forms of this holy violence to whom Jesus promises the kingdom of heaven.

The human being is an aggregation of heterogeneous vital focal points or centers. His physiological energies, sentimental forces, cerebral faculties, metapsychical fluids, find themselves being dissolved in the vase of personality, might

I say. But this complex mixture subsists by virtue of an independent force that, to give it a name, I call the eternal soul. Every part of us, from the mineral skeleton up to these radiant organs by means of which our imagination reaches the spheres of pure ideas, and these invisible suns that are the paradises of knowledge and of beauty, receives the warmth of this divine flame and feeds upon its light. But let us visualize just that part of us which the field of conscience delimits. It is the battlefield of two adverse wills: one belonging to light, the other to darkness. This latter seems the stronger of the two. It almost always wins out in the world. Yet it subsists only by virtue of the first, which is essentially life, which all beings, even death, have need of so as not to sink into nothingness. The physical body bears the marks of this inner combat; it is constantly being oppressed by the influence of the world of darkness, to which it resists only thanks to the force of the world of light. Any act is a prolongation of this combat: consequences perpetuate themselves, for good or evil, according to whether the inner spark that bestirred it came from light or from the shadows.

Among all species of diversified actions, that which belongs exclusively to the human being, that which distinguishes and dignifies him, that which permits him to fully express his inner life, is speech.

From the cry and monosyllable of the primitive idioms up to the infinite shadings of ancient ideograms and of those of modern language as refined by the poets, speech remains the conveyor of Universal Life specialized within the individual, the mobile form of our most characteristic forces—which means the most profound. Speech remains the agent of all communications in spite of distances of time or remoteness of space. In its pure state, speech springs from the center and reaches the centers. It condenses attitudes, gestures, and mimicry. Absolutely receptive to the will, speech either saves or kills, either prevents or precipitates; it illuminates or darkens according to the intention that lies behind it and propels its use.

Hence, to speak is a grave act entirely filled with forces that want to live, and with spirits filled with desire. Our futility, our maliciousness, certainly weaken our words. Our sincerity and kindness exalt and vivify them. That is why the angels of the just Judge count all unnecessary words as dilapidation of a precious substance. That is why our guardian angels register our promises. It is why Jesus, knowing our thoughtlessness, advises us not to take an oath—in other words, not to bind ourselves in indissoluble bonds. Do we not change our minds several times a day? Do we not constantly burn what we have adored?

Now, one of the most potent oaths is the one of conjugal fidelity, which is the alliance of two hearts, two bodies, and two living spirits. To swear by heaven, the earth, or upon our honor means to bind ourselves for the entire time that the witnesses to our promise will last, and doubtless that is very grave. But when two human beings bind themselves to each other, their pact is stronger than any oath, because our human dignity surpasses that of any other creature. According to temporal measurements, stars and demiurges are far greater than we, but according to the eternal scale, we are the kings of creation.

That is why divorce granted by earthly legislation counts as nothing before our soul. That is why in current agreements it is better merely to say yes or no, or to subordinate our promises to God's permission. That is also why, no matter at what cost, we must honor our marriage contract and consider ourselves freed only if the other mate has broken the contract with full cognizance of the fact. Grandiloquent phrases come from a hypertrophy of the self. The disciple makes himself small and fallible, hence he speaks without hyperboles. Words, in his mouth, regain their exact sense; he uses no superlatives. He does not say "It is frightful," for a banal incident; he does not become "literary." Like his Master, he speaks simply, because he knows he is but such a little thing in the immense universe.

Thus, regarding the conjugal promise, which is bound by the monosyllable "Yes" before the priest or the justice of the peace, one could say that, along with all great and grave actions, the minimum of words suffices to tie the knot, because it is great, rare, and inalienable.

⊕

The talion of the Hebrew ("an eye for an eye"), the karma of the Hindus, the reciprocal influence of the Chinese, the rebounding shock of the Hermeticists, the causality of philosophers, all explain the same law of action and concordant reactions that rule the physical as well as the moral world—in short, the entire empire of destiny. Nature is a whole system of forces in unstable equilibrium. Each excess irresistibly calls for an excess in the opposite direction. Otherwise, the whole system would be decentralized. And, as the tendency of these forces is to engulf one another, if the stronger ones continue getting stronger, they cause cosmic cancers. Just as we notice in the behavior of our overly industrialized society, so the whole system crumbles into individualistic pieces. The intervention of an equilibrating force outside and independent of this system becomes the sole remedy against a slow death by dispersion.

This independent force, which Catholic theology calls grace, is the very operation of Christ. This extra-natural, supernatural, non-created, non-conditioned breath fills the voids, realizes the impossible, the unhoped-for, and out of nothing remakes additional life.

Before the gospel, a few sages had foreseen this miraculous force. It is they who introduced into the sacred books of former religions maxims of mercy. But it is Jesus who has given them a soul, an immortal spirit, and out of his own flesh, his own hands, and his suffering, has built for them a terrestrial body equally immortal. It is because of him that men may, at times, surmount the revolts of instinct, surpass even the rigor of justice, and reach up to pardon.

Does not each man receive from the milieu where he lives more than he gives to it? Is not this milieu an assembly of distinct beings? Are not the mutual contacts of one with others the logical incidents from which science or meditation can find some kindred causes? We might say that these incidents that touch us were really meant for us, and that by welcoming and utilizing them, by taking care of them, we fulfill our universal role as best we can. Philosophy, as well as mysticism, teaches that what happens to us is precisely, at that particular time, the best exercise and work for our perfection, and the best contribution we can make toward general perfection.

By neglecting to respond to the unformulated demands of creatures, we are parasites. By responding strictly "to the letter," we are barely doing our duty—we but follow the natural course. But if we want to ascend to the supernatural, we must surpass our duty by imitating the Father, and force ourselves to give more than we receive. (Matthew 5:38–41)

Also, no obligation, no attack, no exigency from beings, ever comes to us without a reason, either according to the ancient thesis that we have been a despoiler, an importunate beggar, in a past life toward those who bother us today; or else, according to the Christic thesis, that this distress and these duties come from God, who imposes them upon us as tests, as progressive exercises, to attain diverse virtues. We must live by accepting, shouldering, and submitting to everything by never giving in to self-pride, rancor, fatigue, or envy; or by satisfying our own tastes. Still, that is not sufficient: our intention must be pure.

To offer the left cheek after having been struck on the right in order to prove the mastery we hold over our emotions, is a sign of pride; to accept being imposed upon by a boor, or performing some other kind act, in order to be liberated of a spiritual debt, is a sign of avariciousness—just greed! Doubtless, acts of virtue produce useful as well as other similar results, but for them to exhale all their savor, for our hearts to waft up on the volutions of their incense, it is imperative that we accomplish them spontaneously, in pure obedience, without thought of self, devoid of any selfish motives.

Only then will heaven pour out its balm within our hell. Our kindness will dissolve angers, our generosity will dissolve greed, our cheer will counteract peevishness. In short, the great secret of the mystical approach to life is that the only way to save one's self is to forget one's own salvation and to concentrate only on alleviating the misfortune of others. Deep in our hearts we are aware of this, and as we progress on the road of renunciation, its voice becomes stronger and stronger, and in measure as we become more humble; heaven in turn enters within us. Thus the true servant takes no pride in the ease with which he forgives, knowing full well that his enemies' resentment can never equal the harm he has done them. Knowing that a vast atmosphere of Mercy reduces the penalties of immanent Justice; that tribulations can never equal our resistance: knowing this, he takes no credit for his submissions or forbearance.

Knowing that his body does not belong wholly to him, he takes care of it and protects it as he would a precious servant that a prince loans his friend; yet still, he knows how to demand its obedience. Finally, he knows that of all the organs of knowledge and action of which his personality is constructed, only the very center of this psychic, intellectual, psychological, familial, social, human person—this center, I say, this feeling of "I," this self-consciousness—belongs to him alone. It is on this nucleus that through the difficult division of the self he will focus the efforts of this heart—all the flames of his love for the divine—so that its nature may be transmuted from tenebrous to luminous, from self-absorbent to radiant, from stingy to generous, even to prodigality.

Violence attracts violence, kindness attracts kindness. Resist the evil you do not want to commit, not the evil you are subjected to. Never be afraid to give. Give all you can of what you have: money, clothes, time, advice, knowledge, even your affection for as long as it is yours to give. The sacrifice that the philanthropist qualifies as useless, is still useful. It radiates the beauty of the superfluous in the eyes of angels; it may even accomplish a miracle. Give to whoever asks of you. If there is an equal need, give to the one whom you do not like, rather than to the one you like.

If someone desires to take you upon a path that is not

yours, take it anyway: all paths lead the true disciple to Jesus. Do not fear evil places, for it may be you bring them light. We all carry the same sordid germs, so let us not approach abject people with high-and-mightiness. What is our virtue worth? Does it not lean upon God's support? Imagine yourself in the place of the vicious man with whom you are speaking: what would you like to hear? What words would touch you without your being hurt? No matter what pains you take for this fallen being, do you not know that heaven has done, or would do, as much for you a thousand times over? It is human to love whoever gives us joys and pleasures, or whoever we sympathize with, but it is divine to love whoever harms us. True love is nourished by privations, afflictions, and hostility. Only that kind of love which comes from God restores harmony and establishes peace. The kingdom of God is neither a symbol nor an abstraction. It is a living, an organic, whole that has been coming closer and closer to the earth for the past twenty centuries, and is closer now than ever (in spite of the horrors we live through)—and that, with imperious authority, our efforts, the slightest word of forgiveness, the slightest gesture of kindness, compel us to keep coming closer. That kind of evocation is far less ceremonious than the mysteries of magic—but far more potent. Imagine this event as best you can: at the advent of heaven on earth, rites are useless, only moral perfection is necessary; there is no sacrifice but that of the self; no incense but that of prayer. In proportion as the human being empties himself of the temporal, so does the divine fill him.

Remember that the Son is always here, attentively awaiting our slightest effort, ready to sustain us when we stumble, happy to pour his very life into the vilest among us at our first request. Let us remember that universally exceptional presence and behave before him as we believe he would behave. For certain, one day, here or somewhere else in the immensity of creation, this presence, now invisible, will become visible. At first these visits will be rare, then more frequent, till at last at the end of duration they will become a state of perpetual union among the splendors of the House of the Father.

Love and wisdom, which the kabbalists and Swedenborg portray as the dual aspect of divine life, may, through our care, take on tangible forms in art, in the family, or society, because they inevitably draw, need, and complete each other. St Augustine exclaims: "Love, and then do as you will." Also Leonardo da Vinci says: "Understand first, then you will love." Both are right, but the former enunciates a superhuman truth. In us, the faculty to love pre-exists the faculty of understanding: not because of what we are today, but because of what we are essentially. That is why those who hate us (since the heart lives mostly upon hate on this earth) dissect us, penetrate our beings, and even disassemble cog wheels of which we were unaware. Their malevolence is of great benefit to us; let us thank them for yanking us out of our faults. Then the love, meekness, and prayer that the gospel asks us to offer for them will be, both for them and for us, of inestimable value. (Matthew 5:43; Luke 6:27–35)

The serenity of nature and its all-precluding munificence, as imposing as they seem to us, are the almost extinct reflection of the prodigality with which the Father gives his children everything that can be of use to them. May they in time do as much for one another and for all inferior beings! May our bountifulness fall as the rains of spring. Grant that our love superabound like the summer sun upon all those who come in contact with us! Our model is the loftiest: the most diverse aspirations of the poet, or the thinker, the artist, or of the proletarian, can contemplate the perfect image of their ideal in Jesus's face. But for them to apprehend it, first they must crave it. We should never sight a higher state without recognizing immediately that we are conscience-bound to attain it, to undertake the great efforts needed for that end. There has to be a fiery enthusiasm coupled to humble abandonment; a most inflexible energy to act coupled to a smiling indifference to success as well as to failure; a suppleness of love that adapts itself to one and all, plus a most rigid tension of the will for the same goal—that is what is needed. The fulcrum of our spiritual equilibrium has to be changed; there has to be a springboard out of the world in order to uplift the world. This particular center of gravity, this mobile though imperturbable equilibrium, is our Jesus. It means having confidence in the Father, and being obedient to the Son.

Our intellect, our mentality, and our instincts, resemble sheep herded into too small a corral. We must give them space, or, more exactly, we must not fear introducing them to the new pastures that Providence offers them. Yes, this state of liberation may bring suffering in its wake: habits must be broken, apathies must be stirred, and we may well have to accustom ourselves to new horizons. But no matter: to grow we must step out, free ourselves; we must understand, take within, suffer, and have compassion for the sufferings of others. Through our physical, intellectual, or sensitive forces we must offer and give everything of ourselves. Our family, friends, strangers, adversaries, and country must all become an occasion for us to shatter our lethargies.

But in our center, our heart must remain firmly fixed in God. To be perfect means to be one in intention and universal in action. It means accomplishing all our tasks with the same ardor because they denote God's will in its innumerable forms. It means focusing the whole life of our spirit toward one goal alone: to serve God, by one sole means—abnegation. In other words, to enter into the kingdom we must force ourselves, conquer all doubts, and surpass the possible. Then power and miracles will descend.

This great work can be realized. The saints have done it within the moral plane. Geniuses have done so within the realm of art and within the realm of thought. The impossible of today is the possible of tomorrow. The kingdom of God is the inexhaustible treasure of all that which surpasses aspiration or human concepts. It is the ensemble of the archetypes of Good, of Truth, and of Beauty. The disciple of Christ has full permission of drawing from it with both hands, because he fetches splendors only in order to share them with his brothers, while retaining the same humble anonymity of which God gives him the perpetual example. (Matthew 43:48, Luke 7:31–36)

Prayer

E SURE you do not perform your acts of piety before men so as to attract their attention; if you do that, you have no title to a reward from your Father who is in heaven. Thus, when thou givest aims, do not sound a trumpet before thee, as the hypocrites do in synagogues and in streets to win the esteem of men. Believe me, they have their reward already. But when thou givest alms, thou shalt not so much as let thy left hand know what thy right hand is doing, so secret is thy almsgiving to be; and then thy Father, who sees what is done in secret, will reward thee.

And when you pray, you are not to be like hypocrites, who love to stand praying in synagogues or at street corners to be a mark for men's eyes; believe me, they have their reward already. But when thou art praying, go into thy inner room, and shut the door upon thyself, and so pray to thy Father in secret, and then thy Father, who sees what is done in secret, will reward thee.

Moreover, when you are at prayer, do not use many phrases like the heathens, who think to make themselves heard by their eloquence. You are not to be like them; your heavenly Father knows well what your needs are before you ask. This, then, is to be your prayer:

Prayer

Our Father, who art in heaven
Hallowed be thy name
Thy kingdom come
Thy will be done on earth, as it is in heaven.
Give us this day our daily bread.
And forgive us our trespasses,
As we forgive them that trespass against us.
Lead us not into temptation (Let us not succumb to temptation).
But deliver us from evil.
Amen.
(Matthew 6:1–13; Luke 11:1–4)

The entire immense creation, from the mass of infusoriae up to those who people the stars, is sustained by the hand of the Father, which is the Son. This incessant, divine, and ineffable holocaust is being celebrated everywhere without any other publicity than the joy of some rare creatures who know how to draw benefit from it. A hundred centuries ago, the Chinese sages said that heaven's activity is secret and that only its results are visible. This anonymity is the very sign of its perfection.

Yes, the disciple of Christ must act as if he were not acting. In a spectator's eyes, he lives, breathes, thinks, works, purchases, and loves just like anyone else; but in his heart he tries to do all of these things without any thought of personal gain. His whole concern is to find what his Friend's will is, and to do it. He is not concerned whether the results will be useful to him personally; he shuns honors, fame, or wealth; he tries to escape from evil; he is convinced that it is the Master who accomplishes good through him as intermediary.

Then, centuries later, when he will have risen from soldier to chief he will have become indifferent to glory or scorn, intelligence or ignorance, successes or reverses. Thus he imitates the perfection of the Father. It is in order that we may reach that state, so that the whole world may feel its ascending march, that the gospel enjoins our prayers and alms to be done in secret.

A seed grows in the field where it has been sown. Even if you sow a poor piece of ground with good seeds, it will alter the quality of the fruits. If you perform any kind act with some personal benefit in mind, no matter how small, the fruits of your act will be spotted with the rust of avarice, sensuality, or self-glory. The self corrupts and ravages still further, but let us stop at the first depredations—we already face hard work.

I repeat, the ideal for which we make the greatest sacrifice—which means our acts—is the one that recompenses us. If you do anything so that people will learn of your generosity, their esteem will be your only reward. You will not receive any from heaven, because your altruism has not been dedicated to it, but to the god of worldly glory instead.

Evil and good are opposites. Evil is a sort of parasite that has in itself the need to grow. It cannot satisfy that need except by vampirizing the living powers that are within reach—and among these powers, the spirit of man ranks first. That is why, in spite of ourselves, we bequeath to our children the evil we have committed. Moreover, many people believe we find it again upon our return to earth, and that that struggle, if we still have the courage of coping with it, is much harder the second time. Good, on the contrary, does not draw its substance from the world. It is life. It feeds upon itself and grows by propagating: on the condition, though, that this propagation be a sacrifice. Good is a light that shines in the darkness; and the darker the night, the more ardent and numerous are the sparks. Hence, if we are the intelligent workers of good, let us sow it without our brothers being aware of it. Let us not broadcast it, so that other beings (less visible beings) will not know it either. As it is impossible for us to behave that way unless we are truly humble, heaven will recompense us (though it owes us nothing), grafting into our heart the little bud of light of which we have been the caretaker. Our discretion does not end there, anyway. Consider this quality, not as a virtue, but as a means, as a working tool. You will apprehend its advantages that much more easily.

Of how many wounds, pains, or quarrels is slander the cause, besides indicating a lack of moral elevation? Criticism attracts criticism; one gossip leads to another; bragging incites a lie, and so forth. But even if it be granted that we are not making spiteful remarks, that we are merely relating what we have seen our neighbors do—why do it? He did not ask us to do so, and by doing so we might even arouse envy, malice, or a judgment. Let us remember that before pretending to do good for others, we must first of all learn how not to harm them. We have the rigorous duty of never hurting anyone. If our acquaintances and friends are for us nothing but occasions for doing evil, let us drop them; let us find others with whom we can do and say something useful.

We must be so discreet that we willfully forget what we have heard about others. To stop tattling is easy; but we must reach the stage where no one may even guess that we know something. Finally, what we have heard regarding another must not influence our inner judgment regarding that person—a judgment we might formulate in spite of ourselves.

⊕

The school of prayer, the practical one, has three courses: anonymous charity, suffering, and temptation. Prayer can as little be learned from books as joy can be, and I do not know if there are twelve men on earth who know how to pray. One finds thaumaturgists of course, and saints; we see them at prayer, and their demands obtain results. But these startling beings are for the most part like sentinels passing on the password without understanding it: they execute an order. Prayer, however, this formidable act of frightful temerity, this incomprehensible and obscure exchange, takes place way beyond here. Yet, if these venerable men do not understand, how could we, mere clay, know? But it is essential nevertheless that our ignorance, our lowliness, our nullity pray.

Some people never pray because either they do not think about it, or because they do not have faith, or because prayer is beyond their ken; all of which may be due to educational background, to culture, or to one's malleable reactions to the tests of destiny. The immaterial organ of prayer is not yet developed in these people, and their consciousness still ignores the possible recourse to invisible powers.

Here is how the development of our consciousness operates: The spiritual man incarnates. He tries to make the physical man aware of the invisible and intelligible realities. If the physical man responds to these attempts, he becomes more refined. He becomes a poet, an artist, a philosopher, or a seer. His nerves become sensitive to delicacy, and his imagination, broadened and cleansed, reflects pictures from the beyond. His will aspires for the ideal, and these movements (which recognized psycho-physiology calls functions) build organs into the finer bodies, organs that in turn vitalize, dynamizing some parts of the physical body. These wheels within wheels cause the changes that any inner crisis operates in the physical body. The spirit thereby sculpts the body. The painter's eye bears a visible sign, and the eye of the saint acquires a very particular quality: the immortal spirit within them has modified their mortal form.

When the yearning of an immortal soul finally tends to the divine (and that always happens at a definite time in its evolution), holy desires are born. Any desire builds around itself its organs of action and its own form of expression. By virtue of this, artists who portray sacred characters give a particular contour to the head of the saintly personages they depict and paint.

The more we defer taking a stand, the harder it becomes; the less we pray the less we can pray. Hence it would be wise to start right away in spite of being lukewarm, in spite of ennui and of lack of response. Any circumstance must serve as a pretext to ask God's help. We never can bother God; never will we exceed doing the ultimate our duty calls for.

Any desire is a hunger. When it is God we hunger for, it is called prayer. But in reality, any desire, even any effort, is a prayer. And in order to be hungry, our forces must be at a low ebb.

Work *per se*, any kind of work, is a preparation for prayer, along with good example; it is the only fruitful and real prayer for the immense majority of men. On this account (and do not be misled in this regard), those we know as contemplatives are not examples to be followed; they are the exception. Nowhere does Christ mention quietude, ecstasy, and spiritual marriage. If I dared scandalize you, I would say they are human embroideries. The duty of man is first of all to live, to act, and to work. Then, if he has spare time, he may devote it to study or to any other art that pleases him: he is free. He can also just stick to his duty, and even surpass it: that is true mysticism. Veritable prayer is a far more complicated action than material work. It demands profound cognition and especially some rare faculties. Hence we must exercise it assiduously.

Beware to whom you are praying: whether you are addressing the living Father, or whether you are invoking a seraphim of intelligence, an archangel of beauty, or perhaps a god of spiritual selfishness. You must understand that the absolute will descend within you only if the relative has been ousted from the field. Drop all intermediaries. However great they may be, they are but creatures at best. They can only loan, not give. Also, what do we know about invisible beings? What certitude do we have that they are really in the true light? If we address ourselves to heaven, heaven will give an order to its children and angels to come and help us without our having to know them, nor having to call them.

⊕

We can pray any place. God is everywhere. It is preferable to do it within the confines of our home, as we are not seen and our attention may be less distracted. But do not believe, as so many sanctimonious people do, that a special place is indispensable in order to speak to the Father. The absolute is above, outside, and within all forms, inaccessible by ritual alone, free of all conditions of space and time. On the other hand, if these rites are useless, not so are the vital radiations of your actions, whose essence these rites try to capture. If you want your room to be pure, make it a temple of the true cult, exercise good therein, do not become angry within it, do not permit the walls to hear useless or malicious words, for everywhere are eyes and ears that listen to and observe us. Let us set good examples even to the beings we consider inanimate. Psychically, you must also lock yourself in your closet and establish an inner silence. Pray aloud, as long as no one can hear you. But see to it that your passions and worries are stilled. God is always within us, even when we do not feel his presence. And the more so when we feel barren. Understand that we must not pray in order to obtain palpable consolations, or to experience more or less agreeable psychic impressions. If you feel such things when you pray, I would almost advise you not to pay any attention to them, because to follow them distracts and leads you to seek after spiritual ecstasies. If heaven grants them to us occasionally, let us accept them in simple gratitude, for it is so easy to be self-hypnotized or to conjure through autosuggestion or magic some long-desired psychic manifestation, and to greet it as from God.

When praying aloud we animate the request, because the voice gives a body to the desire—not an artificial body, such as those produced by perfumes, gestures, diagrams, yantras, mantrams, and psalms, but a normal and natural body. From man's standpoint, the universe is divided into spheres and hierarchies. From heaven's standpoint, these various parts keep a separate existence, even though God reassembles them ceaselessly into the mobile unity of his life. Let us also be a unity like that. When given a task, let our whole being—with its innumerable organs—cooperate, so that that pure intention may bring all these currents, muscles, magnetism, mental tension, fires of desire, spirits, subtle forces, and breaths back to the central harmony from which they spring.

When speaking to God, choice language is useless. There are more pagans on earth than we might believe (Matthew 6:7). I do not mean to imply that Brahmanism, Islam, or Catholicism are wrong in prescribing thousands of invocations to their faithful, but these practices do not lead them directly to the center. In that center there are two parts: the spiritual heart, where divine light shines, and the "remainder," where natural lights shine. Whatever this "remainder" may do, if the heart does not cooperate with it, its exterior energies do not reach God. But then, if the heart acts, the "remainder" is unnecessary.

When a devout man recites prayers for an hour, it is almost impossible for him to keep thinking solely about what he is saying: his words pass into the invisible realm of sound, where they give rise to waves capable of producing an effect upon psychic, or even upon physical, matter. However, heaven has not been reached in this way. And if that devout man is a prodigy of will-power, and if for one solid hour he has unfailingly thought of what he was asking, he has lost fifty-five minutes pursuing what five minutes would have been sufficient to do well.

The same remarks apply exactly to all rites: from liturgical gestures (to which we have been accustomed from infancy), to astrological determinations, to the innumerable observances still practiced in India and China. All these things are crutches to weakness or incitements to indifference. They are useful, but they are mere auxiliaries in the end. Let us not award them the essential role.

Prayer

⊕

How can we make ourselves heard by God? I will merely repeat that essential truths are few, and that one must constantly return to principles and to their application.

The Father of course knows what we need without our asking for it (Matthew 6:8) because he knows everything, no doubt, but above all because he alone is good. But still we must pray. We must pray even when we believe our doing so is something useless. We must do so because praying is an act—because to pray is to obey nature's wish, and to crown universal effort.

Everything prays: the stone that matures in the depth of the quarry, the plant in search of the sun, the animal saluting the sun's daily course. Any act whatsoever is a demand. The result is not obtained through our will only, but because, when working for its realization, our energies, even the most physiological ones, desire and hope for success. Only the human heart (and all too often) believes itself to be master of the world, and rejects any idea of help. And, as our spirit is the supreme flower of the whole of nature, we are obliged to perfect the great work of evolution and link it to the throne of the Father.

This premise being established, let us look for the conditions indispensable for our prayer to be heard by God. God is everywhere. And of all beings, it is he who is closest to us, because he is in our very center. Yet we can be, and too often are, far from him because our heart is dual. In many cases our voice does not reach him because our will does not speak the language of heaven. So we must live according to the law before attempting to pray.

Next, we must be humble. God does not heed the proud, those who believe themselves powerful, clever, or wise. No one, having looked at the vast powers that crush us, or at the immensity of the unknown beyond us, could believe himself to be such. This is the reasonable level of humility, the simplest. Also, we must not believe ourselves to be better or more intelligent than our comrades. This is already more difficult and necessitates a certain knowledge of self (plus undergoing quite a few disagreeable experiences, because only those who have suffered are indulgent).

Rare are the disciples who descend to the third level of humility, the level where one considers oneself to be the vilest of men, the least good, the least worthy of interest: the one wherein one perceives that, as the apostle says, "we have nothing except what has been given us." In truth, humility is a bottomless abyss: one can keep on descending without fear of becoming lost. It is the safest of retreats, and no price should be too steep for us to attain it, because the door is never found at the same place, and one has to constantly wage the fight again in order to pass through it.

The third condition necessary for our demand to be heard is to be on the path of peace. Heaven is the world of peace. We must forgive those who have hurt us—not only men, but all creatures and events, ideas, sentiments, things, and the invisible. We can enjoy this gentleness only if we have confidence that the Father does not send us unjust tribulations. When we want to speak to him, let us forget our worries for the moment. We will then be able to bear them more calmly and combat them better. Forgiveness is the best anesthetic to alleviate our wounded pride.

As a fourth requisite, we must address heaven with a feeling of gratitude both for our joys and for our sorrows: if the joys are periods of rest, the sorrows are our only means of advancement, because we still fear tribulations.

Fifthly, we must pay attention to what we say. This we must do not only intellectually, but perfectly: in our heart and body. This condition is difficult to fulfill. We are by nature inattentive. We waste so much time and speak so many unnecessary words! You will recall that we have already covered this point. Hence, attention is useful primarily so that our demand may prove useful too for the instruction of the invisible audience and of the invisible spectators who surround us: if they see us busily engaged in something else than what we are asking, they do not take us seriously; they go away, and we become responsible for the scandals and errors that ensue. And while persevering in your demands, do not forget to add that God's will be done. Too avid or too enthusiastic a request would introduce into our prayer a ferment of self-will.

This ensemble of conditions must seem rather complicated and possibly difficult to you. But it is only apparently so. On the spiritual plane, more so than on the material plane, everything is related and one. Harness yourself to realize one particular rule and do not take on the next one until you have mastered the first in all of its applications. Your effort for the one will singularly facilitate the necessary effort to control the others. But most importantly, do not think that the results attained were of your own doing! In our ascent toward perfection, our strength, success, and all fruits come from heaven. No matter how great our personal energy may be, we supply nothing but our adhesion to divine succor. I cannot give you general proofs of this, but through observation each of you will find some very convincing proofs, because they will have been experiential.

⊕

Moreover, there is an inner attitude we must adopt and maintain so that it becomes habitual. We must act with composure. God is simple. He loves simple people. He listens to them more willingly. He embraces the humble, the little ones, the poor. This is why mystics affirm that as we eliminate from our heart the relative and creatures (which are obstacles), in that same proportion the absolute, the uncreated, flows into us.

Hence it is sufficient to address the Father with the same candor we used when, as little children, we asked our parents for a favor. The form of the demand is unimportant: we are still so young at this that the most sublime esthetic is gauche and awkward in the eyes of eternal beauty. The legends that portray angels gathering the prayers of the saints in order to carry them from hierarchy to hierarchy up to the throne of God are true in the theological sense of the word. If it is not always angels who fulfill that role, it does not matter, for everything is anticipated and ordained: each thing goes back to its mother; lights return to the light; darkness goes back to chaos. Some prayers go up and some go down, according to their density. The demand rises as high as the purity of the supplicant gives strength to its wings. Men's prayers do not always reach the Father, but if the sphere they reach is too ardent for them, it is quite possible that compassionate beings will gather them, make them their own, and present them to God as if of themselves. That is how our prayers are granted more often than we deserve.

These intermediary beings, whose name or essence it is useless for us to investigate, hear only that which bears the seal of unity. And, should you address your appeals to them, they would understand your desires less than if you addressed God directly. We cannot think without some part of our spirit (etheric, astral, mental, etc.) emanating toward the object of our thought. During this pursuit, many unforeseen encounters occur. That is why, while working on a definite problem, we may incidentally solve another. Also, true prayer is a total withdrawal of our being, which is achieved through perfect calm and profound attention. Hence it is quite natural that while our prayer ascends we may experience peculiar sensations and psychic, spiritual, and even physical emotions. These emotions constitute a stumbling-block, because our nature, bringing us toward those sensations particularly agreeable to us, might lead us to consider them (perhaps erroneously) as signs of divine favor, which quickly leads us to forget the object of our prayer, which is God, and instead willfully focus our attention upon an accidental phenomenon. That is what causes us to relapse into illusions and into what Hermeticists call the astral.

While you are praying, do not stop to analyze, enjoy, or take note of the particular sensations that might come your way. Do not forsake the goal. If mixed or evil beings are the ones sending you these subjective or objective manifestations, you will be better off not letting yourself be diverted by them; if they come from beings of light, these beings will not resent your attention, your remaining focused upon God.

We are terribly far from the absolute. Before reaching there, how many deserts, precipices, and tempests there are in between! So, do not worry about the distractions, arid periods, or temptations that will come as you pray. These are mere incidents during the voyage. Hold your heart steady. If your voice has been heard, it is in this very core of your intimate being that the answer will come. You will rarely catch the words, but you will always experience its exquisite freshness, its charms, and its vivifying, regenerating action. Let us not seek for anything more. Let us render thanks when this favor has been granted us. Let us be thankful also if it has been refused, because in this way our faith will increase.

I do not say that you must scorn all manifestations of the Invisible, no matter whence they come. I only repeat that you must not expect them, or become attached to them. Take note of them just as the scientist notes the reactions in his laboratory. There is a lesson in everything: in visions, voices, breaths, objects being displaced, and quakings. These are levels or planes changing places, coming closer to us; or it might be we who are going to their abode. Do not build systems. If your actions are according to the law, heaven will do everything necessary for you to know truth, even if your duties and responsibilities do not give you enough leisure time to reflect or study.

Prayer is an immense action; the most superhuman of all efforts. Behind each of us are multitudes of people who anxiously await that we open the doors of the temple where they can come to pray. There are some who die from this desire. We are responsible for these sufferings that we barely surmise, however; and yet we all know that prayer is a duty. We are doubly responsible from that moment on, and when we unconsciously satisfy the intense yearnings of these things, our voice becomes for them a harmony, a light, or dew.

Permit my telling you these things. I am recalling them to your memory, but you do not need them to act with rectitude. For, from the beginning God has made man aware of everything material. From now on, you will have less merit in performing your duties because knowledge will have grown you to the detriment of faith, and your responsibilities will be increased if you do not perform them, since you now know something more of the reasons. Believe me, in order to do the will of heaven, and to return to heaven, it is not indispensable to understand everything. Intelligence is a kind of encouragement that God gives us, but it is not an irreplaceable modus operandi. Confidence in Jesus is sufficient. Efforts of will and of meditation are inadequate to convey our demands to the feet of God. Kind acts and purity of heart are the only true vehicles.

After what has preceded, you will understand that the language we use to pray is immaterial. Those who are imbued with theories of esotericism believe that scholarly tongues, Sanskrit, Hebrew, Greek, and Latin, possess a more active power in the subtle atmosphere. What they forget is that everything reaches maturity, its apex of growth, and its decrepitude. Ancient languages once were living. Today, modern tongues are alive, which we must employ, dynamize, and spiritualize. We are born in the bosom of a particular nation because our work at the present time is to be performed among those people. We must not become hypnotized with antiquity. Nature does not recede, it goes forward. What we must do is put the inner light in contact with all present forms of created life. It is useless for us to bother about the astral, the ethers, or secret fluids. The plane about which we are given an inside knowledge is the one that needs our care. Later we will work upon other planes. Let us not look for distant or abstruse things. Let us be content with performing our extensive daily duty, that of the earthy, the tangible. There is a lot more work here than we will ever be able to do.

"Birds of a feather flock together" says the proverb. So it is. It is a fact that any man who duplicates the acts of another unites himself to his protagonist on the plane of his acts. Hence, those who revive the words and acts of Christ, even in the trifling measure of their capacities, if they do it wholeheartedly they are united with him.

For Christ's life is an uninterrupted prayer. He himself is the living incarnation of prayer. He was the pioneer who hewed the passage through which our appeals can rise to the Father. He is the mediator, the interceder, the priest, the victim, and the sacrifice.

Nothing that Our Lord Jesus Christ has thought, said, or done comes from anywhere else than heaven. That is why he is philosophically incomprehensible. Mental concepts cannot grasp the infusion of the absolute into the relative or the effusion from the relative toward the absolute—the double curve of which is they very life of the Savior. That life is the realization of the impossible, the materialization of the invisible, the existence of the inconceivable.

Thus, the model prayer he gave his disciples is not only the expression of the needs of the universe; it is also a statement of the things the Father considers useful to our personal beatitudes, as also to the beatitude of nature as a whole. It is the framework of cosmic movement. It indicates its components, its points of departure, its modes and goals. It represents the army of creatures in its collective ascension and the law of the perfecting of the whole human composite. In short, it is the image of life. Hence, some mystics have rightly discovered therein the rule of extraordinary stasis of individual consciousness, while others have recognized in it the arcana of the creation of the world.

It is St Theresa who developed the first of these points of view most comprehensively. According to her, when the soul has recognized the Father who is in heaven through the methods of human cognition, through the discursive operations of understanding, it enters into the state of abandonment and begins the practice of the prayer of quietude whose phases are described in the first demands of the Pater Noster. The praise "Hallowed be thy name" is in fact a period of rest after the fatiguing asceticism of purgative life and of logical meditation. It denotes the first dawn of contemplative life, when the creature has given almost its all. Then the Creator is going to give it illumination, as if in answer to the second demand, "Thy Kingdom come." Quietude now reaches its level, joy descends into the soul and occasionally communicates itself to the body, which may become the theater of extraordinary phenomena.

When this first phase of relief has been experienced, a new period of work begins, whose third demand, "Thy will be done" establishes the foundations through humility and through the total inner abnegation of the created being. The essence of this work is the assimilation of the divine will by the human will, whose life little by little becomes a sacrifice. This effort causes pains that are the sign of the new birth, of the mystical genesis of the Word within us. That is the "daily bread" from which we receive a crumb each day, such a powerful food and so plentiful that the masses of souls cannot withstand it. Sorrows, trials, persecutions—all imaginable sufferings—are in reality only the effects of this divine remedy upon our inner spirit.

The fifth demand, forgiveness, must become the touchstone of all virtues, the sign of regeneration, the material and objective proof that all parts of our being have assimilated the mystical bread—the living Word.

⊕

But let us leave to the elite souls the mysteries that their exceptional efforts lay bare. Let us keep our feet on the ground where the crowds live—does it not offer us everything that our weakness is capable of overcoming? The best way to recite the Lord's Prayer is to see the words as representing truisms, not allegories or vague abstractions. Examine each of those petitions according to the breadth of its universal domain, and in the depth of its human meaning. Just one of those petitions would suffice to fill your hours with ecstasy, to pour you all the strength you need, and enlighten you with certitude.

The power, wisdom, and kindness that this name of Father evokes, this "turning back" to him that all things should bring us to; his reign on earth and over us, upon all parts of the one and the other; his effective government, which is actual, constant, primarily paternal, and then royal; this will, Christ himself, that we desire to see realized and incorporated into the whole universe, in all of our being; this bread, source and sum-total of the substance of nature; these offenses, committed or borne, from the reign of evil, against which we must wage a desperate fight; these temptations, which are excellent to fashion us and all other creatures into spiritual athletes; and finally, this evil that entices us and that we do not understand, that we must affront and from which only the Father can deliver us!—What a list is this of subjects to ponder over, to admire, and to adore! If we contemplate them with simplicity, what need is there of hieroglyphic symbols, scholarly transcriptions, or rites!

The obscure tasks that are our law are not less arduous than the enthusiasms of speculative mysticism—they are perhaps even more difficult. The Father gives to whom he wants, and what he wants. A sublime person may, in one hour, become an imbecile. Hence, it is preferable only to consider the immediate effort, and to concentrate the whole of our energies upon the present.

Here are a few useful considerations that, at our present state of comprehension, may help us better understand the Lord's Prayer, how to say it as best can be from our heart, uniting us to the One who transmitted it to us.

Our Father

The idea of succor that is born in the heart of man must ascend logically up to the all-powerful Being par excellence. When Christ names God *Father*, it is to make us aware of his infinite solicitude. The God of the gospel is not the vindictive Jehovah of the Israelites, nor the indifferent and impassible *Parabrahman* of the Vedas. Because of the love he bears us, he is concerned about our fate, afflicted by our errors, and rejoices with our wholesome joys. Were our eyes open, we would be abashed at the spectacle of all the beings and forces that God puts to work to give us life, to help us keep it, and to make it increase for us. Instead of chastising us, he watches for the smallest gestures of repentance, so that he may hasten toward the prodigal child and extend his hand to comfort him. Nothing happens during our existence—we do not even take a piece of bread or touch a stone—but that the Father has foreseen it, and judging it good, has permitted it. You know all this of course, but it is good to hear it again, because we often do not dare follow the logical consequences of spiritual intuition—our inner nature takes fright and trembles before the divine lights. So, do listen carefully to the almost imperceptible voice of the Friend who speaks in the center of your heart, and, once having heard it, obey him no matter what.

Who art in heaven

The heaven of the gospel is not a paradise similar to the abodes of rest of the ancient religions. Paradises are nothing but planes of existence more or less superior to the earth and upon which the spirit of man may relax and stock up forces for an ulterior descent into some kind of hell. Thus, according to the belief of reincarnationists, a man who on earth experiences all sorts of joys finds himself in paradise; another, who is constantly in the turmoil of misfortunes, finds himself in purgatory. Any place of existence is a paradise for the one and a purgatory for the other, according to their previous merits. Among those "gardens of delights" are some where beauty, intelligence, and splendor unfold a million times more profusely than on earth. But, though the happiness we might enjoy upon these radiant spheres is as difficult for us to imagine as are astronomical dimensions when compared to those of earth, we only remain a limited time upon these spheres—whereas the absolute, heaven, the kingdom of God, offer us an eternal sojourn.

Heaven is the residence of the Father, par excellence. And if some translators of the Lord's Prayer write: "in the heavens," one must conclude from this that God is everywhere, even in the kingdom of death—that he permits creatures to erect a wall between them and himself, but sees them anyway. For him there are no veils, no barriers, no caverns.

Hallowed be thy name

You might have read about the esoteric adaptations of the Lord's Prayer in scholarly books, where one finds abundant dissertations upon terms found in the Kabbalah (which are more or less similar to the words we use). Do not become overly enthusiastic about these speculations. Among ten authors who treat such subjects, believe me, there is not one who writes from experience. Yes, the *sephiroth* exist, as do all the planes spoken of in the *Zohar*, as well as in the books of the Brahmans, and many others. But it is a very difficult thing to go and explore them while keeping one's psychic equilibrium. It is not that amateurs lack curiosity, but that they lack capacity.

The highest among adepts barely know a thing about the essence of names, or about that of numbers. Do not undertake any extraordinary mental efforts. Conserve your energy for fulfilling your daily work. You will thus sanctify the name of the Lord in a much healthier, more living, more fruitful manner than any kind of meditation. Thus do we offer homage to God, simply acknowledging our nothingness before him and expressing infinite gratitude for his kindness. If there are beings in the world whose shoe-straps we are not worthy to unloose, how evident it is that we are not worthy to lift our eyes to the Father. Never will we thank him enough.

Thy Kingdom come

God is master of the universe about us. But he awaits upon the time when creatures recognize him of their own accord before manifesting his sovereignty openly. In the present state of things, he leaves all visible power in the hands of those who abuse the force he has given them. It is true that this usurpation does not take place without his tacit consent, but he keeps this permanence of his solicitude hidden from men—so that, to all appearances from here-below, it is not his kingdom that flourishes, but that of gods, devils, and men. Hence the children of heaven must desire divine manifestation. In other words, the submission of creatures to their creator must descend little by little from the absolute, to incarnate in each of the regions of the relative: successively in nebulae, upon planets, within subtle forces, animals, plants, stones, and men—in any being, individual or collective, visible or invisible.

The reign of God within man is moral, intellectual, or physiological. The reign of God upon a planet is an organic, social, or physical paradise. The reign of God in the universe will mean its total reintegration. And one of the capital effects of the works of Christ has been to establish here-below the foundation for this divine and beatific sovereignty.

Thy will be done

It is evident that we do not know God's designs directly. That is why we should primarily ask him to accomplish those designs. Since we are intellectually certain of their excellence "by definition" so to speak, we hope to see them fulfilled out of love from their author. In fact, the absolute is not only the impassible, the indifferent, and the impersonal, such as the pantheists claim. To the contrary, since he is the absolute, within him are comprised all forms of relative life—and when he overshadows creatures, he dons the mantle, or assumes the form, of their perfect state of being. In his role as Father of the world, God takes an interest in us in our joys and sorrows, and he likes to see our hands raised toward him. His indulgent tenderness makes him—the all-powerful—seek our collaboration, though seemingly superfluous to his work.

And so, we really have nothing to be concerned about, except to obey the divine wills that concern us: the remainder providential designs God has formulated for us. He makes us aware of them first through our conscience and later through the voices of his envoys. These two codes are sufficient to solve all the uncertitudes regarding any decisions we may have to make. All the rules they contain may be summed up as *charity*. And, as any desire of a created being begins with his satisfying his selfishness, so, no one can help his brother except through inconveniencing the self—to which we must add that doing God's will means smashing our personal desires relentlessly, breaking our self-will, and annihilating the pleasures of the self.

On earth as it is in heaven

This is the corollary to the realization of God's reign. Heaven, as remarked a while back, is the place where God's will is perfectly executed; all forms of life upon that plane are the very forms of his divine will, which live by, and through, it alone. Here on earth, life also comes from the Father in its principle, but in its development is sustained and violated by other nourishments than those of eternity. Hence, on earth, it is essential that the hunger of all beings, and the inner nature of their desire to live, should change.

The Father alone knows the opportune moment and the means by which this conversion may be operated. That is why we ask him that his will be done—given that, being his will, it is perfect. In proportion to men's obedience to God, the whole of nature is healed and liberated. Therefore, the only indispensable lesson is to know God's will. And our only task is to exert all of our energies to that end.

Give us this day our daily bread

Man, relying upon himself, believes he is free, albeit he is but a slave to his passions or desires. From a certain standpoint, these latter are "rattles" that the gods wave before the eyes of our spirit to make us conform to their wishes. And just as any farmer sees after the welfare of his servants and animals, so do these gods take care of us and meet our wants. But the food they give us is not always healthy; often enough it is too stimulating and corrodes our organism. Only the bread the Father intends for us to have is good.

What is this bread, and where do we find it? Everything has been prepared in advance, so that the food necessary for our physical body may be given to us. If a few find it with difficulty, there must be just cause for their misery, perhaps a cause that is better for them not to discover, or even to know. We are here on earth to learn, and, among other things, to undergo material tests. We have no warrant for judging anyone but ourselves. As for the foods for our other bodies, our astral, subtle, mental, psychic bodies (or whatever other names esotericists may give these bodies, and no matter their number)—these also are prepared before our birth. Hence, subtle influences, flames, sentiments, ideas, and inspiration come to us according to our desires and according to our need as requisite for our work.

Yet all these things are merely the nourishment for the envelopes of the spirit, and for the spirit itself—which in turn is nothing but the vehicle of the soul, nothing but the wood that sustains the eternal flame flickering in our very depths. This flame that languishes in exile in this dark world seeks for something akin to it, for something that carries a reflection of the absolute, of liberty, and of the supernatural. Thus, it is only the bread of divine life that we should ask from the Father. And what in creation is divine par excellence, if not love, if not sacrifice?

Without losing hold of your equanimity or your reason, please understand that our being is very vast. All of us, even the loiterers, are kingdoms. To everyone, the immense universe sends voyagers. The basest of our acts have unforeseen reactions—and that particular act may be, upon the cosmic ocean, the last ripple of a stone thrown from a billion miles away. Besides, there are all sorts of sacrifices that family, social, and intellectual life bring to us in addition to those brought up from the living depths of our own being. All that stirs in the recesses of our subconscious and ends by forcibly and finally making us perform acts whose true cause, as well as whose true sense, escape us—all this is divine love, as well as suffering, for our nature.

Hence, suffering is a grace, a favor, a benediction. Whatsoever that suffering may be, it is a sign of love. It is the bread of heaven, and the disciple avidly accepts it, for it is through this suffering that our union with the great Sacrificed One is perfected. It is by its materialization that suffering builds the human nature of the man of God—it is through this that we find again the paths that his venerable feet had trod.

What is the life of this body of flesh? It is both an assimilation and a dis-assimilation proportionate to terrestrial matter. The lives of our other bodies follow an analogous process. The life of our soul is the absorption of divine life, and divine life is Our Lord Jesus Christ. What did he do? He gave himself to the world, not mentally only, or with subjective compassion, but *really*: through flesh and blood, with all that existence entails. Within our small capacity, let us do likewise. Let us give others of our time, our money, our ease, our happiness, even to the whole of ourselves. The inconveniences that will ensue for us (inconveniences that may extend from a least bother to the worst anguish) will be part of the eternal wheat germ.

To help us in our inconstancy, our task is parceled out. Is there a man who can plan his life in advance, even but one year in advance? On this account is it written "sufficient for the day is the evil thereof." A day is a life, in fact. It is like a parcel of earth. It is a work, a complete act. We have to begin and end each day by a return to its author, to the nocturnal mystery. That is why Jesus asks, with us, only for "our daily bread."

Forgive us our trespasses

We have already spoken at length about forgiveness, but might I remind you that to obtain forgiveness from God, we must exercise it too. In so doing, we imitate Christ, and he takes us along with him. In the first instance, we learn to forgive when we remember universal justice, and then by remaining in the extremity of humility. Once these passive and subjective exercises have been followed, we can practice the most superficial sort of forgiveness, which is the forgetting of an injury by the organ that received it. Then and only then can we speak this petition of the Lord's Prayer without condemning ourselves.

As we forgive those who trespass against us

This divine pardon is not an exchange. It is a recompense for our willingness to embrace meekness. The other translation of this demand, which speaks of the remission of debts, offers the same meaning. Whatever attack we are subjected to is an acquittal of debt: and disobeying God's law is always the contracting of a debt. In order to speak out this petition, we must not fear hearsay, ridicule, or ruse.

Lead us not into temptation

These words (giving the Vulgate's exact translation) were not spoken by Christ. He permitted them to fall into usage, however, because they minimize the idea we have of the power of the devil, and also encourage the lukewarm. Christ said, do not let us succumb to temptation. In fact, temptation properly speaking comes from the Adversary and with the permission of God, as is clearly described in the book of Job. There are two kinds of temptations: those that come from our personal perversity and are the result of the alliance of a devil with one of our forces (these being the most common temptations and least difficult to overcome), and those that come from a direct visit of a soldier of evil, which are rarer (these being reserved for men who are already strong). Resisting temptation is doing good work, perhaps one of the best of works. For we cannot withstand the assault without being humble, without confidence in God, or without a struggle. Thus, all of our powers are put to work. Our spirit and our personality become a battlefield whereon the seven forms of evil ceaselessly combat the seven forms of good. To triumph, calmness, steadiness of mind, and decisiveness are essential.

Have you observed visitors at a zoo teasing the goats and monkeys, and how, when the animal finally rebels and lurches or screams, the teasers are satisfied and stroll away? They have in this way taken out part of the evil they had within themselves, or else perhaps the patience of the butt of their meanness has worn them down. Now, there are beings about us also who are more indulgent and stronger than we. In like manner, they also tease us. Although to us our sufferings seem horrible, desperate, and infernal, to them our struggles are cause for mirth. But when, having reached the end of our rope, we cry "Let us not succumb to temptation," then along comes a guardian who pushes the teaser away, making him ashamed of his wickedness.

So, when temptation crosses our path, the first precaution to take is to remain calm. Do not get flustered. What seems large is so small in comparison to the grandeur comprised in the world. If you are a soldier of heaven, you will withstand the attack patiently, and will not ask the persecutor to go away.

Deliver us from evil

We want to be cured of the universal evils of physical disease, ignorance, selfishness, social destitution, ugliness, cruelty, and every sort of compulsion. As I have often stated, we cannot be delivered by ourselves. A man who ceaselessly puts on a display of heroic virtue is neither cured nor enlightened by his virtue. His works are no more than a gesture or a demand. The Father saves him, rather, because of active prayers. I repeat, God does everything in us. All we can do is to place ourselves in the best attitude so as to profit from his gifts by asking him to enlighten our discernment, in spite of its weakness.

Amen

Amen, and the gnostic kabbalistic formula by which we sometimes end the Lord's Prayer are self-explanatory. It is an act of faith, without which nothing is obtained or accomplished. We already have had, and later will again have, occasions to speak about faith.

The Spiritual Abode

f you forgive men their transgressions, your heavenly Father will forgive you your transgressions; but if you do not forgive men theirs, neither will the Father forgive you your transgressions either. Moreover, when you fast, do not appear gloomy, as do the hypocrites who assume a sad countenance so that men can see they are fasting; believe me, they have their reward already. But thou, when thou fasts, anoint thy head and wash thy face, so that thy fast may not be known to men, but only to thy Father who dwells in secret; and thy Father, who sees what is done in secret, will reward thee.

Do not amass treasure for yourselves upon earth, where there is moth and rust to consume it, where there are thieves to break in and steal it; lay up treasure for yourselves in heaven, where there is no moth or rust to consume it, no thieves to break in and steal; for where your treasure is, there will your heart be also.

Sell what you have, and give it in alms.

The lamp of the body is the eye; and if thy eye is clear, the whole of thy body will be lit up; but when it is diseased, the whole of the body will be in darkness. Take good care then, that this light which is in thee is light, not darkness.

No man can serve two masters; either he will hate the one and love the other, or he will devote himself to the one and despise the other. You cannot serve both God and Mammon.

I say to you: Do not fret over your life, how to support it with food and drink; over your body and how to keep it clothed. Is not life itself greater than food and the body greater than clothing? See how the birds of the air never sow, or reap, or gather grain into barns, and yet our heavenly Father feeds them; are you not more advanced than they? Can any one of you, for all his anxiety, add a cubit's growth to his height? And why should you be anxious over clothing? See how the wild lilies grow; they do not toil or spin; and yet I tell you that even Solomon in all his glory was not arrayed like one of these.

If God, then, so clothes the grass of the fields; which today lives and is cast into the oven tomorrow, will he not be much more ready to clothe you, men of little faith? Do not fret then, asking, what are we to eat? or, what are we to drink? or, how are we to find clothing? It is for the heathen to busy themselves over such things; you have a Father in heaven who knows that you need them all. Make it your first care to find the kingdom of God and his justice, and all these things shall be yours without the asking.

So, do not worry about tomorrow, for tomorrow will bring worries of its own. Fear not, little flock, for it is your Father's good pleasure to give you the Kingdom.

Judge nobody, and you will not be judged. As you have judged so will you be judged by the same rule; condemn nobody, and you will not be condemned; forgive, and you will be forgiven. Do not judge on appearances; but judge according to justice. You judge according to the flesh; I judge no one.

Give, and it shall be given unto you; a good measure pressed, shaken, and overflowing will be given you in your bosom; for the measure you award to others is the measure that will be awarded to you.

How is it, that thou can see the speck of dust which is in thy brother's eye, and are not aware of the beam which is in thy own? Hypocrite! Take the beam out of thy own eye first, and so thou shall have clear sight to rid thy brother's eye of the speck.

You must not give that which is holy to dogs. Do not cast your pearls before swine, for the swine may trample them underfoot, and then turn on you and tear you to pieces.

Let us suppose that one of you has a friend to whom he goes at dead of night, and asks him, "Lend me three loaves of bread neighbor; a friend of mine has come to me after a journey, and I have nothing to offer him." And suppose the other answers from within doors, "Do not put me to such trouble; the door is locked, my children and I are in bed; I cannot bestir myself to grant thy request." I tell you, even if this man will not bestir himself to grant it out of friendship, he will get up because of his importunity and provide him with everything he needs.

And I say the same to you: Ask, and you shall receive; seek and you shall find; knock and the door shall be opened to you. Everyone that asks will receive; that seeks, will find; that knocks, will have the door opened to him.

Among yourselves, if a father is asked by his son for bread, will he give him a snake instead of a fish? Or if he is asked for an egg, will he give him a scorpion? Why then, if you, evil as you are, know well enough how to give your children what is good for them, is not your celestial Father much more ready to give, from heaven, his Holy Spirit to those who ask him?

Do unto others that which you want them to do unto you, because that is the law and the prophets.

Strive to enter by the narrow gate. It is a broad gate and a wide road that leads on to perdition, and those who go in that way are many indeed. But how small is the gate, how narrow the road that leads on to life, and how few there are who find it!

Be on your guard against false prophets, men who come to you in sheep's clothing, but are ravenous wolves within. You will know them by the fruit they yield. Can grapes be plucked from briars, or figs from thistles? So, indeed, any sound tree will bear good fruit, while any tree that is withered will bear fruit that is worthless. That worthless fruit should come from a sound tree, or good fruit from a withered tree, is impossible. Any tree which does not bear good fruit is cut down and thrown into the fire. I say, therefore, that by their fruit you will know them.

> The good man out of the good treasure of the heart produces good, and the evil man out of the evil treasure produces evil; for it is out of the abundance of the heart that the mouth speaks.
>
> Not everyone who says to me, "Lord, Lord," will enter the kingdom of heaven, but only the one who does the will of my Father in heaven. On that day many will say to me, "Lord, Lord," did we not prophesy in your name, and cast out demons in your name, and do many deeds of power in your name? Then I will declare to them, "I never knew you; go away from me, you evildoers."
>
> If anyone comes to me and listens to my commandments and carries them out, he is like a prudent man that would build a house, who dug deep, and laid his foundation upon a rock Then a flood came, and the river broke upon that house, the winds blew but could not stir it because it was founded upon a rock. But the man who listens to what I say and does not carry it out is like a man who built his house in the sand, without foundation; when the never broke upon it, it fell at once and great was that house's ruin.
>
> When Jesus finished speaking, the multitudes were astonished at his teaching because he spoke with authority and not as one of the scribes.[1]

As we treat our brothers, so the Father treats us. (Matthew 6:14) Consequently, when we want to obtain a particular

[1] Matthew 6:14–34, 7:1–29; Luke 12:33–34, 11:34–36, 16:13, 12:22–32, 6:37; John 7:24, 8:15; Luke 6:41–42, 11:5–13, 13:24, 6:43–44, 6:46–49.

favor from him, before expressing our desire we should show him our good-will. We should prove in some way that we will accept his decision, whatever it might be, by depriving ourselves of something agreeable or useful for the benefit of another who lacks that thing.

All religions prescribe various kinds of fasts. You are aware of the mechanism. Life is a wheel that turns—each of its spokes or rays occupies, in succession, the place of all the others. If one of these rays wanted on its own to accelerate or slacken speed, there would be a rupture of rhythm, unless it offered a compensation. In social economics this system of exchanges is called commerce, in physiology it is called therapeutics, in religion, sacrifice.

In a sphere alive with known radiations and functions, one could formulate a science of sacrifices by means of appropriate experiments: one could determine how the suppression of a particular energy engenders another particular energy. The transformation of forces is not a modern discovery. Prehistoric initiations knew that heat could become light, and that certain psycho-physiological forces are convertible. Such is the source of the ancient doctrine of correspondences and signatures, which is the basis of the secret sciences of antiquity. The fragments that remain from these secret sciences naturally seem vague and hypothetical to contemporary scholars. Yet this method has the advantage of permitting the spirit to search for resemblances and thereby reach a conclusion of daring syntheses, whereas analysis, which only collects dissimilarities, multiplies an accumulation of specific perspectives and prevents the philosopher from having a bird's-eye view of the whole. Analysis and synthesis are two operations of thought that should not exclude each other. If by making us wear blinders the first gives us precision, the second provides stops along the steep road of knowledge that grant the intellect enough time to take a second breath and gather the courage to go on further, after having had the satisfaction of classifying the results thus far acquired.

The ancient sages used this dual method to study all beings, whether invisible or physical, individual or collective, abstract or concrete. They would arrive at such conclusions by means of esoteric practices, proceeding from experiment to prudent hypotheses, from hypotheses to more daring experiments. Particularly in the field of practical psychology, they would lop off some particular human energy by means of a precise precept of asceticism, so that another energy could increase that much more—for the same reason a gardener prunes a bush. This alternate approach was possible at the time because the dynamic wheels of the world were turning in a direction, and at a speed, that were known. Little by little, the cleverly solicited superior forces would descend faster, and reciprocally make the inferior forces faster ascend. This was the regular procedure used in the colleges of Nabis and Tongsangs in Benares, as well as in Nineveh, in Thebes, in Delphi, and in the Celtic lands, as well as among the Atlanteans. But all this culture of artifice could be effected only within the closed orb of temporal nature. Christ, on the other hand, by laying a new path across nature, from the kingdom of the Father down to the lower depths, has turned everything upside down, infinitely multiplying the finite power of sacrifice and opening up previously non-existent paths to ultimate liberation. But men must follow the path he shows them.

In his religion, which is all spirit and truth, there is no more need of priest or victim. It is he, Jesus, who is the temple, the priest, and the holocaust—all at the same time. And each disciple, in the measure wherein he imitates his Master, shares this same prerogative.

Let us examine the corporal fast. When the body is deprived of a particular nutriment to which it is entitled, the cells of this nutriment suffer, because they are subjected to a delay in their evolution. On the other hand, the reserve cells in the body rush to fill the physiological lacunae produced by this fast—so they sacrifice themselves and die for the general good of the organism. The sufferings of these two categories of elements, and the intention for which we make this fast, direct them into the Invisible, where they become auxiliaries for the realization of the desire of the ascetic—they give a subtle body the superior force he hopes to bring down.

No matter what the privation is, the mechanism is analogous to it. The more severe the need, the more intense the pleasures. The greater the suppression, the more subtle or elevated they are, and hence the more active will be the dynamism of that abstention. The more idealistic the purpose of this abstinence is, the more effective it will be. Thus, more forces will emanate from the suppression of an aesthetic pleasure than from the giving up of a meal, and still more from the suppression of a passion, and so forth.

Any self-imposed moral, intellectual, or psychic abstinence borne to help one of our brothers furnishes active agents for this spiritual succor. But of course we mustn't make a deal with God. Let us not tell him: "If you grant me this, I'll do that..." First, we must offer our privations and say: "Whether you grant me this or not, I shall not murmur, nor be discouraged: you know better than I what is best for me, or my brother, for whom I have fasted."

On the other hand, we owe our body the food and sleep it requires. That is why a fast is licit only if our intention is devoid of any selfishness. Later, when we will have paid all our debts, when we are free, we will have legitimate command over both our body and over nature.

Thus, a gospel-inspired fast differs in its intent from one done for esoteric training. The true disciple forgets himself, and would, if need be, neglect his own salvation so as to bring help to one of his brothers. Another important item Christ recommends is that we must not publicize the good we do. Let no one learn of our fasts. We must learn to show a smiling countenance constantly, even when subjected to the worst ordeals. If sadness becomes unbearable, hide away to weep, lock yourself in your room so that none but God see you sacrifice. This is the only path that leads to true faith. Man can be recompensed but by two masters: the prince of this world or the Lord of heaven. All that belongs to the world—fame, praise, success, admiration, and temporal joys—are but recompenses from the prince of this world. The recompenses from the Lord of heaven remain secret. That is why his friends are generally unknown and held in little esteem by men. In short, do we not complain and speak of our unhappiness because our faith in God is too weak, because we find his burden too heavy, or because we judge ourselves with too much indulgence? It should be sufficient for us to know that the Father sees us and loves us ceaselessly. (Matthew 6:14–18)

⊕

"Earthly treasures" are the recompenses distributed by the prince of this world. Jewels, fine furniture, and luxury are a part of this treasure, as are also success, fame, renown, and public acclaim. Thieves can take such treasures away from us. Even the glory of a celebrity can suffer an eclipse. But if we seek happiness in stable joys, then we must look for it only in what is stable and immutable. And what is stable and immutable, if not the eternal?

How can we take root in this fixity? That is our most difficult task. It is more difficult than the conquest of an empire, though if the divine dwells in us, it is the simplest of gestures.

The psychology of the gospel is very simple. First, it indicates that within man is a central fire, the source of free-will, the prime mover of all our conscious movements, and as well of some of the most important activities of our unconscious life. This fire is fed by a spark of the uncreated light that is the seed of the Word inside of us. The simple fact of living keeps this fire ablaze: living according to the law of Christ purifies it until it reaches the high degree of incandescence and brightness. Now, since the growth or stuntedness of the entire personality depends upon its state of being, the one indispensable task is to purify our heart—and the unique method for this task is to purify the motives of our endeavors.

If a man's endeavors are toward a natural goal (such as fortune, glory, and knowledge), when he leaves the earth (recalling that nothing really dies) the self of this man will go into the invisible world, whose terrestrial forms he has coveted. Nothing created remains permanent: everywhere, even in the most scintillating stars, there are thieves, parasites, and destructive vermin. The kingdom of God alone has and procures immutability, certitude, and safety. Since it is intention that changes the quality of desire, of thought, or of any act, we should work only for heaven, by obeying and serving it alone. For if we merely work to *gain* heaven, there comes immediately the fatal risk of mystical selfishness.

A disciple chooses the way contrary to men's customs: instead of trying to make money, or amass unproductive wealth, he seeks to give whatever wealth he may possesses (Luke 12:33). It is through his heart that man is great; it is through his heart that he will someday become the king of creation; it is through his heart that the Adversary succeeds in worming his way into the rest of nature; it is through his heart that non-human beings can attain their own salvation. The heart is the eye of the soul. It is the core of the affections, of the temperament, and of the understanding. The heart is to the spirit what the eye is to the body. It is through the eye, or rather by the quality of its expression, that a man's spiritual dignity or indignity may be evaluated. In our time the heart is sick. Its light is turbid because we use our ingenuity to give it impure foods, so that our eyes seem dull or cloudy. Were we to make our heart clean and splendid, as Jesus asks, our total personality—the empty house still awaiting its mysterious proprietor—would become resplendent with the calmest, kindest, and most limpid light. (Luke 11:35)

Man is one: his spiritual heart confers a living homogeneity to his whole personality. Man's life must also become one; his love, one; his ideal, one; his work, one. Since we cannot even extend our arm without this central vestibule being part of the gesture, neither can we pursue several spiritual objectives at the same time. Any action of terrestrial man is interpreted in the central world of the beyond—which is the very world of the incarnated Word—by the progress of the spiritual man toward the invisible place where resides the ideal that inspired this action.

No more than the body can go simultaneously to Berlin and Rome, can our spirit go toward two ideals at the same time. The popular saying is: "one cannot chase two hares at the same time." For a work to be well done, we must give it our whole attention. And if it is impossible to think of two ideas at the identical second of time, so much more impossible is it to perfect two ends at the same time.

Besides, it is far more difficult to hoodwink the invisible overseers of life than it is to outwit the boss or the office manager. We cannot run with the hare and hunt with the hounds; neither can we serve no one. Even those who believe neither in God nor in the devil live selfishly for themselves alone—by which very fact they serve the devil. Even those more metaphysically-minded, who believe they can escape any servitude by taking refuge in the non-doing attitude (absolute cessation of desire) of the Orientals, become in spite of themselves the most active slaves of the Prince of Darkness—because the hidden desire of the Adversary is that he wants to be, and that he is, the immobile. All creatures, even the greatest, have been born on this earth only to learn obedience. We must choose; and once the choice has been made, we must give ourselves to it totally.

We are quite far from the state of indolence and inertia that unbelievers believe to be the state of the true Christian. (Luke 12:22) When Jesus advises us not to worry, when he furnishes us the example of the birds and the lilies, his exhortation (the most touching and profound that any poet ever penned for his friends) ends thus: "Make it your first care to seek the kingdom of God and his justice, and all these things shall be yours without the asking." A bird finds his and his little ones' food because he fulfills his function of being a bird completely. And the lily, which tomorrow will be cast into the fire, also receives its food and a splendid raiment, because it fulfills with all the power of its roots and leaves its function as a flower. But as for man, his own function is not to build, fabricate, speak, or be in business: these are the outer forms of his functions. His characteristic function is to seek and to realize the kingdom of God, which means accomplishing God's law, and obeying Christ. Whoever attempts living that way is fully aware of the trouble and difficulties it entails. So, man must fulfill just that for which he has been put on earth, and then there will be added unto him...

The duty of a master places upon him the obligation of providing for the servant's needs. And the higher he is in the spiritual hierarchy, the more confidence may the servant have of this provision. Hence, we certainly can abandon ourselves blindly to the Master of masters—the Father—as soon as we have accepted being his servants. Such is the school of faith. Doubt brings to a stop both terrestrial help and divine succor. Faith stays its path through any thicket. It pierces through the walls of all impossibilities. Its cultivation, of course, demands great care; but long before it has reached its complete development, faith gives us proofs of its power by the miracles it lays at our feet.

For the growth of faith, there is no cultivation more efficacious than simple everyday life animated by love. Our life and our body are its instruments. Do not fear that they will ever fail you. If you use them for a good purpose, the Master will take care of them. Is not the approximate hour of our death already inscribed? Let us simplify our needs, wear what we have, eat what is put before us. The less we inject our personality into the details of our existence, the better will the forces and things that Providence has destined for us, reach us. The mechanism of these destinations was sought by the ancient sages. Christ, however, has completely transformed it, so that in our day it is almost impossible to analyze it. Moreover, this science would prevent the surging of faith in us. Christ came particularly to leaven the seed of *faith*. Because, only when the adhesion of our conscience to indemonstrable events is joined to the destruction of the idea of the impossible (which is *hope*) and to the transmutation of selfishness (which is *charity*)—and by these three superhuman movements alone—will we be permitted to land upon the eternal shore from where we sailed centuries ago.

If we wish to be incorporated into the ranks of children of God, we must live only to accomplish the will of God, without any hope of personal reward. In return, the Father meets all of our needs, material as well as intellectual. The true child of God, the one whom God has so to speak created anew, knows everything without study and can do everything effortlessly. The proverb says: "God helps him who helps himself." To help oneself means doing our utmost. And as for "impossible": God takes that in hand. For the disciple, everything comes from God: the people he meets, the events that present themselves, the words addressed to him each moment that he lives, all are signs of God's will where he is concerned—they are the outlines of his new duties and the occasions for him to prove his zeal. By complying cheerfully to the demands of life, he finds peace, and from these contacts spurt the fountains of grace. The Divine Manifestation is ever-present, everywhere; the more we believe in it, the more forces it pours into us—not because our belief creates it (as the pantheists claim), but because our faith hews a passage through the rock of matter and of common mentality.

Divine love manifests itself through all creatures who knock at the door of our conscience, at each moment of the day. These successive visions of successive divine wills are the very fires of sanctification. The less one understands, the more one enters into faith. And yet we should do our utmost to understand, as if reason were our only guide. But, even were we to remain plunged in the darkest of shadows, our confidence should not vacillate one iota. The only remedy to lassitude, obscurity, disgust, despair, and droughts (whatever be their cause) is to let go, or to abandon, oneself to God.

When we do our duty, our worries should cease, because God is good. (Matthew 6:28) "Fear not, little flock, it has pleased the Father to give you the kingdom." This does not mean that the disciple will inherit the kingdom, no matter what he does, whether right or wrong, but that he will inherit it because, no matter how fine his actions are, no matter how heroically he performs his tasks, man's eternal heritage is of such inestimable value that no human effort, no matter how worthy it may be, can ever compare with it: therefore, this heritage remains always a gift, a gratuitous grace.

⊕

For man to be born anew, all the inclinations of the "old" man must have been violently restrained. Each struggle—tenacious, incessant, and bitter—hidden under the cloak of a thousand disconcerting forces, demands that we analyze ourselves thoroughly. We must outwit the maneuvers of our faults and vices. We must constantly invent and find new outlets for our energy. How can we achieve this if, primarily, we do not deliberately tear ourselves from the soil at the contact of which the giant of selfishness finds a brand new force with each misstep? First of all, we must be kind and humble. The first kindness is never to hurt anyone; the first humility is never to believe ourselves better than anyone else. Jesus has told us that in two words: "Judge not."

Simple common sense proves him right. We are all different, one from another. Each of us has a particular destiny and our own personal means of expression; each reacts according to his own viewpoint. Had we been in our neighbor's shoes, might we not have done worse? No entity knows another in the full sense of the word, unless that soul has already followed the same line of evolution as the other. Actually, for us, to judge does not mean to compare or classify—it means criticizing and condemning. By judging, we narrow our spiritual perspectives, we evoke and bring upon ourselves the cause of failures that were not aimed at us and for which we are not prepared—we leave our own path to tread the path of the other person whom we are criticizing. So, immanent justice will treat us as we are treating him, and it will cause us to be caught in the identical snare, to commit the same blunder, and to be guilty of the same fault. From that it ensues that we encounter detours, suffering, and a thousand superfluous occasions of being mistaken again and again.

We must even forbid ourselves the mute criticism that the tongue does not formulate, but that our arid heart engenders silently. What others do is none of our concern. To each his own road. We can only judge from appearances (John 7:24) since, even if we were exactly informed of the details regarding the actions of our neighbor, we could not install ourselves in his soul, in his conscience, or in his body. We judge after our earthly fashion. (John 8:15) He alone who *could* judge according to the Spirit, which means according to truth, he judges no one.

Only the sorrows for another should move us. So, do leave the divining sciences and superfluous curiosities aside. Apply instead to know yourselves in depth by probing for the entanglements of selfishness within yourself. This study alone is sufficient to fill your meditation hours—and you will quickly leave your neighbors alone. Moreover, if we did not possess avariciousness, self-pride, or anger, we would not see it in others—and the faults to which we succumb the easiest are the very ones that are important for us to combat. In fact, slander ranks first among the faults Christ warns us against, and speaks of so often.

Not only should we not misuse our speech; we should use it well, and for good. All truths are not good to tell; discretion is an important quality, for which we do not exert sufficient effort to acquire. Ten times a day we relate what our neighbor has said or does, while being all unaware of the wrong we are doing him, or of the evil we propagate in this manner.

As far as teaching others is concerned, that is a most delicate task which demands more knowledge than eloquence. A discourse uniquely logical does not reach the spiritual center of the auditor. One should first make certain that the latter possesses the germ of profound truths before imparting them to him without risks. To give a spirit a light prematurely hurts him more than a wound would hurt his body. To communicate holy things to those who cannot conceive them is a sacrilege, and the risk for them is to pervert that light and use it for evil purposes. One must not convert people in spite of themselves. The teaching given by example is far less dangerous and can be used safely by anyone. If you attempt to preach to a free-thinker, he will become more stubbornly entrenched in his own viewpoint. But if he sees you devote yourself without thought of personal gain, accept ingratitudes, and meet tests with calm, he will be convinced of your sincerity and wonder about the power of the ideals that propel you. He will thereby of himself do the preparatory work of reflection, and his heart will automatically open, without shocks. (Matthew 7:6)

Our speech reaches within our auditors the same psychic center as the one within us from which it flowed: it reaches the instinct, if our speech is instinctive; the intellect, if it is mental; the heart, if it is emotive. The latter is the most alive—hence, the most powerful. In any case, do not assume the attitude of master. Speak only about that of which you are convinced. Do not proclaim hypotheses as certitude before speaking—pray. Prepare your words by diligent purification, then God will do the rest: he will whisper what is good to tell; he will imbue your discourse with persuasive force. Thus your auditors will not waste their time listening to you, a time for which you are held responsible; and they will assimilate the lights useful for their needs.

You will not meet these requirements unless you are humble. If our body does not spend its energy, we have no appetite; if our intelligence does not recognize that it really knows nothing, it remains closed to the new ideas that God would want it to hear. God is always ready to help those who believe themselves to be small, ignorant, and weak. Keep on asking God, importune him always for all things good (Luke 11:5–8). Because no one really knows how to pray, the spiritual organ of prayer is atrophied. How many months of physical exercise does it take for a puny child to strengthen his torso and muscles? The growth of man's spirit demands still more perseverance.

Do not ask gods or intermediaries. They might grant your prayers quicker, but there would be a debit against you that you would come due later: capital plus interest. Only ask God, Christ, or the Virgin. That is what is meant by "knocking." Keep on seeking; shoulder responsibilities; spend your energy to help others, and your intelligence to ferret evil out of its labyrinths straightaway—which means, go to the end of your rope. As long as the Father has not granted your prayer, continue asking, even for years, because often we do not know what we are asking for. Very often what we ask for would be harmful to us, and often the delay God subjects us to is to permit us to ripen with time, to make us able to appreciate and utilize the gift he is most anxious to offer us. Moreover, no effort is ever useless: the smallest gesture, the tiniest syllable of our prayers is never lost. The Father will always give us what is the most profitable to us. (Matthew 7:11) It is up to us to ask from him only that which may become for us a source of beatitude and strength. And to our ardent supplications, let us add the formula of confidence: "Thy will be done; not mine." The response to such prayers, no matter what the intentions might be, will come from the Holy Spirit. (Luke 11:13) Our whole and complete life must always be entirely geared toward heaven—that is how the powers and innumerable faculties of which we carry the seeds will increase. It is by smithing that one becomes a smith. Not that our efforts are worthy of a salary, but because, by doing our duty, we are strictly giving back to nature what she has loaned to us. But when we do our duty through love and obedience to Christ, he pays us back a hundredfold with such incorruptible tender as the Father has given him complete disposition of.

⊕

Planets, suns, stars, paradises, hells, all the abstract and concrete worlds, communicate with one another by routes that constitute a sort of skeleton to creation. These routes are immutable—only the beings who travel over them change. These voyagers eventually follow the routes that seem easiest to them; hence, the most crowded ones are naturally the widest and smoothest. Any being who listens to his likes and preferences, who wants to travel in comfort with the least of inconveniences, takes the main road. But this love of ease and comfort, this sprawling of the self, leads but to the kingdom of selfishness. And so, the more commodities we have, the more we want to have. One need only take a train to observe that fact. Then, from one demand to another, one reaches a sort of idolatry of pleasure that withers the heart and leads to the gates of death. But if you want to travel toward life, you must take the short cuts, the seldom trodden paths, where the grades are steep, where quagmires abound, where there are no inns, and but a few gendarmes to protect you. So, train yourselves for long hikes; withstand hunger, thirst, and solitude. This solitude is excellent, because nothing stands between the traveler and the Great Pilgrim of the Universe. It is doubly excellent, for there one meets only the envoys of the Father, and because where beings are scarce, angels are more numerous; and also, because where material life is precarious, there also spiritual life abounds.

There are some hidden pathways over which perhaps one

voyager per century travels. A time will come when you will be one of these pioneers from heaven. But for the moment, let us be content to make ourselves small, to be satisfied with the mere essentials on the common road where providence has launched us. You will achieve, by stepping aside for another, by taking a backseat, by choosing the most difficult task, by submitting to the malevolence and the trespasses aimed against you. One must reach the state of loving the newcomer sufficiently so as to extricate him from his load as soon as he asks for it, and even before he does, if you notice that he is timid or exhausted. Do not wait for some heroic occasion to present itself; start by the simplest of sacrifices. It is by accumulating a great many little efforts that one becomes capable of accomplishing the great ones. (Luke 13:24)

This doctrine as taught by Jesus is the only true one. Nowhere else, not even in the radiant worlds dreamed of by the poets, where creatures whose power and beauty would strike us with oppressive admiration, have any truths more complete and more veritable been promulgated than those of the gospels. So, do not rush and follow adepts, seers, or supermen before examining the fruits of their teaching. Your reserve will not offend any of the servants of God.

There are going to be more and more thaumaturgists—they swarm at times of crises. The source of their power is rarely pure. It springs most often from the light of this world, from the spirit of this world, and from the prince of this world. Let no miracle startle or surprise you. Is not heaven able to do all things? Does it not always leave a free field to the Adversary, since from the excess of evil a greater good always ensues? Notice under what name these thaumaturgists act, see whether they employ coercion—for coercion against any being is illicit. Do not follow protocols of training the will. Leave aside hypnosis, autosuggestion, psychic experiences, and magic. Even if you found a willing subject, do not subjugate anyone to that role. Do you not know that an invisible world exists, animated by a thousand unknown forces and peopled by innumerable hierarchies? And does not the physical world offer you a field vast enough for any of your activities? (Matthew 7:15)

If you enter into forbidden worlds, you will bring them nothing but disturbances, and you will bring back trouble. Destiny will then oblige you to begin the work over again, either through an incarnation of atonement, or through expiation—which Catholicism attributes to purgatory.

We barely know that part of our being of which we are conscious. Our unconscious part is still unknown to us. So prudence recommends that we do not introduce any disorder within ourselves under the pretext of developing transcendental powers. For example, to be normal and legitimate, clairvoyance should be spontaneous and not artificially produced. The more the heart becomes luminous, the more refined becomes the body, the more sensitive becomes our nervous system to subtle vibrations, the wider grows the field of our conscience—this is the only licit path. In order to see or to act from a distance, the child of God has no need of placing himself in a secondary state: he knows hidden things while remaining fully conscious of the physical realm.

Moral purification alone enables the spiritual seeds to grow healthily. Everything comes from the heart. The equilibrium of a machine depends on its center of gravity. The heart alone brings light or shadow to our acts. It alone heals or corrupts its surroundings, whereas science, no matter how important it is, is never but an image of things—and a virtuous ignoramus is closer to heaven than is a perverted scholar. (Luke 6:43)

This is where the gospel states, for those who can hear, the great arcana of alchemy, of macrobiotics, and of other esoteric sciences. We too will hear it—later, when we will have become incapable of doing anything else but the will of God.

⊕

In short, good intentions are not sufficient. Acts are indispensable. Unless it is founded upon works, no asceticism is viable. (Matthew 7:21; Luke 6:46) How many men commit iniquities while invoking the name of the Lord! All that which is born from self-will (not only magic) is false. Self-will grabs instead of waiting for heaven to give. The good it does has only an appearance of good, but multiplies evil at the antipode of its gesture. And the more intelligent is the man, the deeper his mind, the more evil he can do by materializing into formulae the scraps he has been able to glean from the free-flowing currents of the spirit.

At rare intervals, God gives a certain power to some of his servants. Among those who look at them, a few—either through envy, cupidity, or indiscreet zeal—try to find ways of reproducing those spontaneous miracles by artifice. This is the origin of all occult arts. These foolhardy people, through vanity or through their presumptuousness, may take the name of the Lord, of Christ, in vain, and thereby constrain some invisible being to obey them. The meaning of the gospel may be perverted; its maxims might be inverted and be used to bind consciences instead of liberating them, to fascinate naive people and satiate covetousness.

Beneath perfect simplicity, the teachings of Christ hide the most terrible mysteries. I am only permitted to speak of them in general terms. But while we are studying them, we must beware of pride; and quite often we must plunge into the tonic depths of humility. A few among the foolhardy ones to whom I referred search with sincerity and benevolence, yet they only succeed in constructing mirages and phantoms. We live on the physical plane. It is in the physical that we must work. Our school is in the physical. But someday, when our self will receive a more subtle body, when it is born upon a more ethereal world, it will be with that particular ether that we will have to tangle. And it would be wrong for us at that time to want to renew contact with terrestrial matter, for in doing so we would be committing the same error as those around us who in their desire for knowledge are now attempting to captivate the invisible.

It is by accomplishing with good will and simplicity the tasks that befall us daily that we prepare for ourselves, after death, this mysterious house of which Jesus alone speaks to us. (Luke 6:48) A man who does not concern himself about heaven also builds a house for himself, but he does so in the created invisible, in the kingdoms of wealth, temporal glory, or relativistic science. But in the kingdom of Christ he will be without a roof, alone, erring like the demons of nefarious loci shunned by human beings. A man who is content with good intentions builds himself a home in the luminous kingdom, but it is a flimsy one, and the onslaughts and storms from the invisible will wreck it. Only the man who acts in God builds for himself a house upon a rock, the eternal rock—Christ who is the immutable Stone—and his future will be forever assured. If we acknowledge successive lives, we understand that each of them prepares for the next one, both in its formal design and in its essential quality. If we accept but one lifetime, realizing the teachings of Christ through works and acts leads to this certain and indestructible life known as paradise.

By examining ourselves according to the most rigorous conscience before acting, by driving evil from us, even from its secret folds, by purifying our motives—finally, by working with all the might, intelligence, and love we possess—we follow the method the gospel suggests, the only method that can be applied with full certitude in any and all circumstances.

The overall study of the Sermon on the Mount is ending here. Christ is now going to pass from theory into practice. St Matthew stresses, conclusively, the affirmative tone that his Master used when he taught. This sovereign authority leaves no room for dubious subtleties—it is far more impressive to the auditor than eloquence. Jesus in fact is the first—unique among all religious revelators—who does not relate things he has had to learn. He knows all things from eternity. Nothing that happens in the universe is unknown to him. In one glance, he penetrates the creature he is looking at and probes its depths—whether it be a star or a stone, whether it be an infusoria or the regent of a constellation. The Father communicates all his projects to Christ, since the infinity of divine action is the Word. Thus, the humble disciple prostrates himself before the words of his Lord, which neither ignorance nor ill will have been able to alter in essence—no matter what exegetes might believe. The disciple studies, or rather, contemplates these words. Through them, he adores the One who pronounced them. From them, he receives, via a communication superior to intelligence, ever-renewed, boundless virtues. Thus does the stature of we servants develop in various forms—but always in increasing plenitude of lights, of forces, and of beatitudes.

Finis

www.ingramcontent.com/pod-product-compliance
Lightning Source LLC
Chambersburg PA
CBHW021402090426
42742CB00009B/958

* 9 7 8 1 5 9 7 3 1 2 2 9 5 *